Environmental Technology Innovation and ESG Investment

Sumiko Takaoka
Editor

Environmental Technology Innovation and ESG Investment

In the Asia-Pacific Region

Springer

Editor
Sumiko Takaoka
Faculty of Business Administration
Seikei University
Musashino, Tokyo, Japan

ISBN 978-981-99-9767-1 ISBN 978-981-99-9768-8 (eBook)
https://doi.org/10.1007/978-981-99-9768-8

This Springer imprint is published by the registered company Springer Nature Singapore Pte Ltd.
The registered company address is: 152 Beach Road, #21-01/04 Gateway East, Singapore 189721, Singapore

Paper in this product is recyclable.

Preface

The relationship between economic growth and the environment has been controversial for over a century. However, frequent natural disasters such as flooding, storms, and wildfires, which cause direct damage to firm assets and supply chains, have made it economically reasonable for firms to reduce their carbon footprints. Therefore, appropriate climate risk management is an urgent requirement for corporate managers. Environmental, Social, and Governance (ESG) investing—in which the investor considers the firm's ESG performance, along with financial information such as profit margins and cash flows—has become increasingly popular in financial markets when making investment decisions. This trend seems irreversible, as climate change intensifies climate events; thus, investors are required to integrate ESG aspects into the evaluation of firms.

ESG investing has its origins outside Asian countries, in the United States and the United Kingdom. Where ethical investing is concerned, some companies that violated religious ethics were excluded from investment when religious organizations managed funds. Unlike this type of negative screening, ESG investing covers all individual firms, and its importance has been emphasized globally in recent years. The current interest in ESG investing, not only in academic literature but also in public policy, is the motivation for launching a research project entitled "ESG Investment Strategies for SDGs in the Asia-Pacific Region."

In April 2006, the United Nations proposed the Principles for Responsible Investment (PRI) because the existing investment decision-making did not adequately reflect economic, social, and environmental sustainability. The PRI comprises six principles for responsible investments that incorporate ESG issues into investment practices. This PRI requires investors to consider ESG factors when selecting investments, to the extent that they do not violate fiduciary duties. In Japan, the scale of ESG investments has expanded—partly because the Government Pension Investment Fund, the largest pool of retirement savings in the world, signed the PRI in 2015 and started ESG investments in 2017. ESG investment, which focuses on the stock market, was expanded to include corporate bonds. Against this backdrop, investors now assess corporate ESG activities more strictly than ever before. However, some investors find it difficult to evaluate how corporate ESG performance would have any bearing on corporate debt, which is supposed to, eventually, be repaid.

Despite a great deal of research on the association between ESG issues and corporate financial performance using United States or European markets, there is relatively little literature on the subject in Japan. There is currently a keen interest in societal needs and social sustainability. This book, therefore, aims to provide empirical evidence and insights into their relationship in the Asia-Pacific region. Regarding the financial markets, the research focuses on the bank loan market, corporate loan market, and credit default swap market in Japan.

Accelerating innovation in environmental technologies is a promising direction for mitigating climate change by reducing carbon footprints and transforming society to be more environmentally friendly. We expand the scope of our research to the Asia-Pacific region to examine the relationship between environmental technologies, migrant inventors, environmental technologies, and CO_2 emissions.

This collection of essays is the product of a research project entitled "ESG Investment Strategies for SDGs in the Asia-Pacific Region," which is sponsored by the Center for Asian and Pacific Studies (CAPS) at Seikei University, Tokyo, Japan. The contributors to this collection were project members and their collaborators.

The project officially started in April 2021, but preparations for this project started in 2020, amid the COVID-19 pandemic. The project comprised members from Australia, Italy, Japan, South Korea, and Switzerland. Because of the preventive measures and quarantine policies, we had to work on the project on a network. With the cooperation of the members, we were able to carry out the project successfully.

I would like to thank all the project members and their collaborators who joined forces on this project during the pandemic. We are also indebted to Megumi Suto, Yukiko Hirao, and many others who commented on our drafts. We appreciate CAPS for its financial support and constantly flexible response to the changes caused by this pandemic. Lastly, I am grateful to the editorial staff of Springer Nature, on behalf of the project members, especially Yutaka Hirachi, for his dedicated support in publishing the book.

Musashino, Japan Sumiko Takaoka

Contents

Background: Environmental Technology Innovation and ESG Investment in the Asia-Pacific Region

Sumiko Takaoka

Today, we face the momentous and global challenge of mitigating climate change without harming economic growth. Climate change and economic growth are mutually related. This is because a company's impact on the environment through its own activities will eventually cause climate change; in turn, corporate assets themselves face the risk of climate change. The physical risks resulting from climate change, such as coastal erosion, floods, and storms, can be substantial for firms that are located or own assets in coastal areas. Even if firms do not have physical assets in coastal areas or countries, their businesses can be damaged physically by climate change through interruption of operations and disruption to supply chains driven by frequent extreme weather events, sea-level rise, wildfires, and changes in temperature and precipitation patterns. In addition to physical climate risks, firms are exposed to increases in various costs, including insurance premiums and resource costs. Moreover, certain sectors impose environmental regulations, policies, taxes, and technological changes to adapt to and mitigate climate change when the society needs to transition to a lower-carbon economy. Firms that operate in such sectors face a transition risk, which is another critical type of risk.

Against this backdrop, environmental, social, and governance (ESG) investment—in which investors consider firms' ESG performance—has been expanding. Global firms are required to implement ESG strategies, particularly to reduce greenhouse gas (GHG) emissions, so that the global temperature rise is limited to two-degree Celsius by the end of the century.

There is also a growing consensus among corporate managers that risks arising from climate change are material to the economy and corporate sustainability. In contrast to the era in which Friedman (1970) stated that businesses' social responsi-

S. Takaoka (✉)
Faculty of Business Administration, Seikei University, Tokyo, Japan
e-mail: takaoka@bus.seikei.ac.jp

S. Takaoka (ed.), *Environmental Technology Innovation and ESG Investment*,
https://doi.org/10.1007/978-981-99-9768-8_1

bility is to increase profits, today, social responsibility is essential for firms to become sustainable in the market.

As consumers in society become more concerned about the environment, firms can achieve higher sales from environment-friendly products or services. This will motivate firms to advance environmental technology creation. Thus, firms will respond to consumers' environmental preferences as well as be motivated to innovate more environment-friendly technologies (Aghion et al. 2023).

Furthermore, corporate managers recognize that the corporate performance of ESG activities impacts investors' decision-making in financial markets. ESG-conscious investors are willing to select and support companies based on their evaluation of the companies' ESG performance.

Therefore, this book focuses on environmental technology and financial markets in the Asia-Pacific region. This region includes traditional and emerging innovative countries such as Japan, China, South Korea, and the U.S. Thus, it covers both developed and emerging countries, which have gained attention not only because of their economic growth but also for their high rate of environmental technology innovation. The research presented here focuses on the nexus between the innovation of environmental technologies, finance, and ESG. Accelerating the innovation of environmental technologies is a promising means of achieving a sustainable society. Accordingly, the chapters of this book address several important issues.

The map in Fig. 1 depicts the total occurrence of disasters worldwide between 1990 and 2021, based on data from the Emergency Events Database. The darker red shading indicates a larger total number of disaster occurrences in a country between 1990 and 2021. Countries shaded in the darkest red are located in the Asia-Pacific region. With respect to climate-related disasters, including droughts, extreme temperatures, floods, storms, and wildfires, countries in the Asia-Pacific region suffer severe damage primarily from droughts, floods, and storms. Moreover, countries in the Asia-Pacific region have been struck by various types of disasters; for example, occurrences of wildfires have been prominent in Australia and the U.S. Diversity in the types of disasters occurring in the Asia-Pacific region are partly based on the countries' geographic factors. Accordingly, these countries engage in particular categories of environmental technology creation to address their needs.

This book makes the following contributions. First, it sheds light on the corporate credit markets in Japan, namely corporate bond and credit default swap markets. The rapid expansion of ESG investment necessitates empirical investigation of the effects of these markets on financial markets (see, e.g. Hong and Kacperczyk 2009; Borgers et al. 2015; Bolton and Kacperczyk 2021). Although ample literature exists on the relationship between corporate CSR/ESG performance and performance on the stock market, studies on the relationship between ESG performance and the corporate debt market are starting to increase in number. For example, Stellner et al. (2015) show a decreasing effect of better CSR performance on credit spreads for Eurozone corporate bonds and Jang et al. (2020) suggest a similar effect of high environmental scores for small firms in Korea. Apergis et al. (2022) find such a decreasing effect at the time of corporate bond issuances. In this context, we address gaps in the literature on the corporate credit market and ESG issues in Japan.

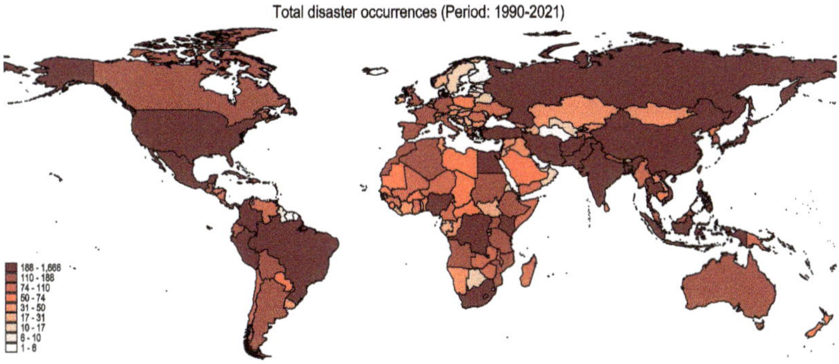

Fig. 1 Global occurrence of disasters *Notes* The data are taken from the Emergency Events Database. Darker red shading indicates a higher number of total disaster occurrences in a country between 1990 and 2021

Second, in addition to the corporate bond and credit default swap markets, this book offers empirical evidence of the relationship between corporate GHG emissions and corporate loans in Japan. This analysis reinforces the contents of this book by incorporating the bank loan market in the comprehensive analysis of corporate debt and ESG issues because the Japanese economy has been characterized by a corporate loan market based on tight banking relationships, see for example Ito and Hoshi (2020). This analysis provides insight into the extent to which ESG issues penetrate the corporate debt market in Japan.

Third, this book reveals the nexus among the determinants of environmental technology, environment technology creation, and GHG emissions in the Asia-Pacific region. It helps identify differences and patterns in the manner in which environmental technology innovation affects GHG emissions and what drives environmental technology innovation. As the Asia-Pacific region is the core of innovation creation in the world, we expect that the evidence presented in this book will enable the reader to improve their understanding of the vital role of this region.

In the following sections, we describe the features and trends in GHG emissions, sustainable finance, and environmental technology creation in countries from the Asia-Pacific region, followed by a brief overview of the book.

1 GHG Emissions in the Asia-Pacific Region

GHG emissions are not equally distributed across countries or sectors, or even within countries. Figure 2 shows the top 20 fossil-fuel GHG emitter countries between 1971 and 2018, where the amount of GHG emissions is divided into three periods—1971–1986, 1987–2002, and 2003–2018.

The top five GHG emitter countries between 1971 and 2018 were the U.S., China, Russia, India, and Japan. The patterns of fossil-fuel GHG emissions by country

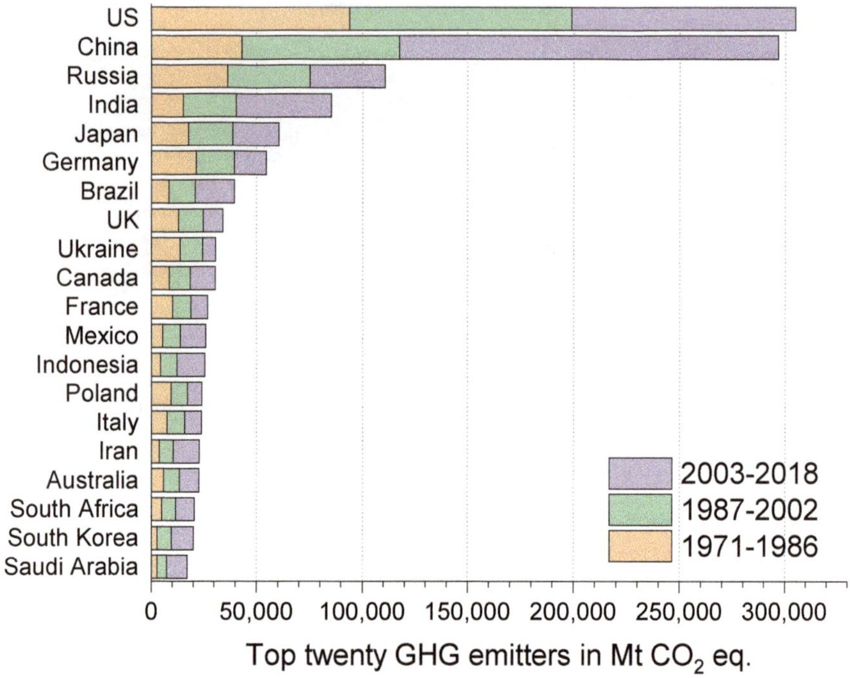

Fig. 2 Fossil fuel GHG emissions by country between 1971 and 2018 *Notes* The data are taken from the Emissions Database for Global Atmospheric Research. The emissions by France also include those by Monaco. Greenhouse gas (GHG) emissions comprise fossil carbon dioxide (CO_2), methane, nitrous oxide, and fluorinated gases

across the three periods in Fig. 2 differ substantially. China has become the largest emitter in recent years. Developed countries have been producing significant carbon emissions by burning large amounts of fossil fuels in energy sectors and/or expanding their economic activities; residents' use of automobiles has also contributed to this. However, in response to warnings about global warming, which causes climate change, developed countries have attempted to transition to low-carbon economies by transforming their energy systems. In contrast, the GHG emissions of China and India during 2003–2018 were much higher than those during 1987–2002, primarily because of the expansion of their economic activities as emerging markets and large populations.

As Fig. 2 indicates, the Asia-Pacific region—comprising the top emitter countries, the U.S., China, India, and Japan—has a critical impact on global GHG emissions and thus has the potential for climate change mitigation. As this region consists of both developed and developing countries, the contributions of their sectors to GHG emissions and composition of the energy sources within these countries differ.

For example, according to the U.S. Energy Information Administration, China is the top energy producer and consumer globally, where the primary source is fossil fuels; in 2021, coal constituted 70% of China's primary energy production and 58% of its primary energy consumption. China continued increasing coal production by 6% in 2022. Moreover, the U.S. uses and produces many different types and sources of energy. The primary energy sources include fossil fuels (petroleum, natural gas, and coal), nuclear energy, and renewable energy sources. The largest end-user sector in the U.S. is transportation, accounting for 36% of the total in 2022. Further, in India, the second-largest coal producer globally in 2021, coal continued to account for most (44%) of India's total energy consumption. With its growing population and modernization, India faces a growing energy demand. Japan, without sufficient domestic energy resources, was the top importer of liquefied natural gas in 2022. Its primary energy consumption has declined gradually over the past decade.

Thus, energy sources and future energy demands differ across countries in the Asia-Pacific region; however, two issues are important. One is financing to facilitate social issues, in particular, the transition to an environment-friendly society. Sustainable finance accounts for ESG considerations when making investment decisions and provides funds for investments into sustainable economic activities and projects. Firms with such projects can access sustainable financing to support their corporate operations while reducing their environmental impact. Second, a promising direction for climate change mitigation and adaptation is accelerating progress in environmental technology creation. Despite the trends in the innovation categories, facilitating environmental technology will lead to a low-carbon society and bolster economic growth while reducing GHG emissions.

2 Sustainable Finance in the Asia-Pacific Region

The momentum for sustainable finance continues to grow globally, as shown in Fig. 3. When the prosocial activities of a firm or manager do not reflect in investment decision-making, the firm's goal is to maximize its profit. Against this classic view, firms now have an incentive to operate their businesses with a prosocial attitude toward ESG-conscious consumers and investors.

The right panel of Fig. 3 shows the amount of assets under management and the asset owner assets under management in trillion USD, indicating an increasing trend in responsible investment. The left panel of Fig. 3 shows the development of sustainable investment assets in 2016, 2018, and 2020 by region, using the compound annual growth rate for 2014–2020. The data were obtained from Global Sustainable Investment Alliance (2020). While Europe's sustainable finance amount declined in 2020 due to a change in the measurement methodology, Australia, Canada, Japan, and the U.S. displayed a consistent increasing trend. Among them, growth in sustainable investment assets in Japan is notably high. Since Japan's Government Pension Investment Fund, the world's largest pension fund, became a signatory to the United Nations Principles for Responsible Investment on September 16, 2015, ESG issues have become critical criteria for investment decisions in Japan.

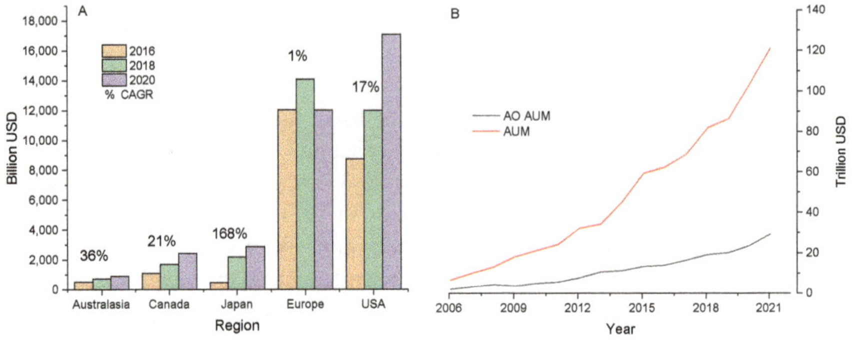

Fig. 3 Development of sustainable finance *Notes* Data are extracted from the United Nations Principles for Responsible Investment website and Global Sustainable Investment Review 2020. AO = asset owner; AUM = assets under management; CAGR = compound annual growth rate

The trend in sustainable finance in the Asia-Pacific region is characterized by consistent strong growth. As the proportion of sustainable investment relative to the total managed assets increases further in this region, firms access to funds for transitioning their business into an environment-friendly one will improve, thus leading to a low-carbon economy. Global Sustainable Investment Alliance (2020) reports that the proportion of sustainable investment relative to the total managed assets is 62% for Canada, 38% for Australasia, 33% for the U.S., and 24% for Japan.

3 Environmental Technology Creation in the Asia-Pacific Region

Countries in the Asia-Pacific region are innovative in terms of patent creation, as listed in Table 1, which contains the number of patent applications filed in at least two intellectual property (IP) offices worldwide from among the IP5.[1] In addition, their growth rate of environmental technology innovation is higher compared to their overall patent applications. The highest growth rates are observed in Asian countries. The number of environmental patent applications in South Korea increased by almost 13.4%, versus an 8.6% growth in overall innovation. Moreover, environmental patent activities in India and Singapore increased at a slightly higher pace than their overall patent applications growth rate; these activities are occurring at a very high pace in absolute terms. China is the only country with a lower growth rate for environmental patent applications than the overall growth rate, even though both rates (25.8% and 26.5%, respectively) are the highest compared with those of other countries.

[1] The five IP5 offices are the European Patent Office, Japan Patent Office, Korean Intellectual Property Office, U.S. Patent and Trademark Office, and National Intellectual Property Administration of the People's Republic of China.

Table 1 Environment patent application dynamics in the Asia-Pacific region

	Environmental patents			All technologies patents
	Compound annual growth rate	Applications		Compound annual growth rate
Country	1998–2018 (%)	1998	2018	1998–2018 (%)
Asia-Pacific				
Japan	5.43	2,797	8,054	3.25
USA	4.56	2,466	6,022	1.82
China	25.82	35	3,495	26.45
South Korea	13.41	282	3,495	8.57
Canada	4.11	200	449	2.08
Australia	2.34	101	160	1.87
Singapore	11.99	11	103	9.92
India	13.27	8	94	10.57
New Zealand	2.71	10	18	1.24
Thailand		0	17	11.49
Malaysia	2.46	4	7	8.39
Philippines		0	2	13.48
Indonesia	3.53	0	1	−1.58
The others				
Germany	3.69	1,778	3,669	0.82
France	4.93	484	1,268	1.32
UK	4.75	312	790	1.10
Denmark	8.40	81	405	3.37
Italy	4.28	169	390	1.57
Netherlands	5.19	135	370	2.38
Switzerland	3.58	169	342	2.78
Sweden	3.79	148	312	1.40
Austria	4.70	90	227	3.20
Finland	4.92	73	190	0.53
Belgium	4.95	64	168	2.95
Spain	7.45	38	161	4.31
Israel	7.06	37	144	4.06
Norway	4.87	40	104	2.10
Russia	7.83	15	67	4.49
Ireland	8.02	13	59	7.49
Brazil	11.28	6	53	6.63

Notes Data are extracted from OECD.Stat.

Even though not all innovations are patentable, when we focus on the Asia-Pacific region, the number of patent applications for environmental technology is much higher than that for other regions. In 2018, the top two innovative countries in the Asia-Pacific region were Japan and the U.S., with 8,054 and 6,022 patent applications, respectively, for environmental technology categories. In contrast, the top two innovative countries in Europe were Germany and France, with 3,669 and 1,268 patent applications, respectively. In addition to these traditional innovative countries in the Asia-Pacific region, emerging innovative countries such as China, India, and South Korea show high growth rates in patent applications for environment-related technologies, with compound annual growth rates during 1998–2018 of 25.82%, 13.27%, and 13.41%, respectively.

These facts indicate that the Asia-Pacific region is a driving force of environmental patent creation, and would remain so with traditional and emerging innovative countries gaining a global share of environmental technology creation. Regarding the beneficial effects of technology and technological knowledge (i.e., technology spillover), the Asia-Pacific region contributes to global environmental technology innovation. Thus, through spillovers and the evolution of environmental technologies, this region plays a key role in ensuring compatibility between economic growth and sustainability.

4 Brief Overview of the Book

This book aims to provide insights into the nexus between innovation in environment-related technologies, finance, and ESG. Accelerating innovation in environmental technologies and promoting a firm's ESG activities that are better aligned with its business and sustainability constitute promising means of achieving a sustainable society. Thus, the chapters of this book address several important issues.

In the following chapters, this book provides empirical evidence by focusing on two key issues related to ESG (particularly the environmental aspect)—performance and its impact on corporate debt. The book examines how capital markets and lending banks evaluate corporate ESG performance, particularly carbon emissions, and clarifies the determinants and outcomes of environmental technology creation. There is a growing body of literature on ESG investments and environmental technologies. By focusing on the Asia-Pacific region and, especially, emphasizing on the Japanese market for the corporate debt analysis, we provide useful and practical evidence based on detailed and extensive data on Japan. Moreover, the chapters pertaining to environmental technologies analyze the broader coverage of countries to better describe the potential of the Asia-Pacific region for climate change mitigation.

The remainder of the book is divided into five chapters. Chapter 2 empirically analyzes the relationship between corporate ESG performance and corporate bond spreads in Japan. It concludes that corporate ESG performance significantly decreases corporate bond spreads, and the effects of ESG performance increase with the recognition of the importance of ESG investment, regardless of the ESG pillar considered. Chapter 3 explores the corporate environmental impact ratio of pricing firm-level credit default swap (CDS) spreads in Japan. Results obtained from the firm-level CDS spreads support the environmental-risk hypothesis. CDS spreads for firms fall in the speculative-grade rating category, regardless of the direct or indirect environmental impact ratio. Thus, the impact is heterogeneous across credit quality. In Chap. 4, Takahashi and Shino investigate the effect of GHG emissions on bank loans using bank-firm loan data for Japanese listed firms. They conclude that loans to high GHG emitters, in terms of level and intensity, are associated with lower loan growth rates, and the effect is economically significant.

Regarding environmental technologies, in Chap. 5, Lee and Han analyze the impact of environmental innovation on carbon dioxide (CO_2) emissions in 26 Asian countries by classifying them into high- and middle-income countries as well as high- and low-effectiveness countries. They indicate that environmental innovation reduces CO_2 emissions; in particular, environmental innovation in high-income (vs. middle-income) countries is more effective in reducing CO_2 emissions. Finally, Chap. 6 discusses the relationship between international migrant inventors and environmental innovation in the Asia-Pacific region. It concludes that innovation in environment-related technologies increases with the stock of immigrant inventors when the country of origin specializes in the production of environment-related technologies.

References

Aghion, P., R. Bénabou, R. Martin, and A. Roulet (2023). Environmental preferences and technological choices: Is market competition clean or dirty? *American Economic Review: Insights 5*(1), 1–20.

Apergis, N., T. Poufinas, and A. Antonopoulos (2022). ESG scores and cost of debt. *Energy Economics 112*, 106186.

Bolton, P. and M. Kacperczyk (2021). Do investors care about carbon risk? *Journal of Financial Economics 142*(2), 517–549.

Borgers, A., J. Derwall, K. Koedijk, and J. ter Horst (2015). Do social factors influence investment behavior and performance? Evidence from mutual fund holdings. *Journal of Banking and Finance 60*, 112–126.

Friedman, M. (1970). The social responsibility of business is to increase its profits. New York Times Magazine, September 13.

Global Sustainable Investment Alliance (2020). Global sustainable investment review 2020.

Hong, H. and M. Kacperczyk (2009). The price of sin: The effects of social norms on markets. *Journal of Financial Economics 93*(1), 15–36.

Ito, T. and T. Hoshi (2020). *The Japanese Economy* (Second edition) MIT Press.

Jang, G.-Y., H.-G. Kang, J.-Y. Lee, and K. Bae (2020). ESG scores and the credit market. *Sustainability 12*(8), 1–13.

Stellner, C., C. Klein, and B. Zwergel (2015). Corporate social responsibility and Eurozone corporate bonds: The moderating role of country sustainability. *Journal of Banking and Finance 59*, 538–549.

Sustainability and Credit Spreads in Japan

Tatsuyoshi Okimoto and Sumiko Takaoka

1 Introduction

The rapid expansion of environmental, social, and governance (ESG) investing raises a question vis-á-vis if the asset prices reflect the firm's ESG performance. Early empirical research related to the relationship between corporate social responsibility (CSR) and financial performance shows mixed results. For example, Derwall et al. (2005) report that the stock returns of companies with higher CSR standards tends to be higher. Similarly, Eccles et al. (2014) report that higher-CSR companies significantly outperform their counterparts over the long term, both in terms of stock market and accounting performance. In contrast, Humphrey and Lee (2011) find no significant difference in performance between socially responsible investment (SRI) funds and conventional funds in Australia. Likewise, Managi et al. (2012) confirm the quite similar performance of the SRI and conventional indexes for the US, UK, and Japan, even if bear and bull markets are distinguished. In addition, Kitzmueller and Shimshack (2012) state that there is sparse evidence that environmental performance enhances financial performance.

Despite the mixed empirical findings of the performance of ESG investments, recent research highlights instances of outperformance for stocks/portfolios aligned with higher CSR/ESG standards during periods of crisis. Notably, Nofsinger and

This chapter was published in *International Review of Financial Analysis*, Volume 91, Okimoto and Takaoka (2024), Sustainability and credit spreads in Japan, 103052, Copyright Elsevier, Reprinted with permission.

T. Okimoto
Faculty of Economics, Keio University and Research Institute of Economy, Trade and Industry (RIETI), Tokyo, Japan
e-mail: tatsuyoshi.okimoto@gmail.com

S. Takaoka (✉)
Faculty of Business Administration, Seikei University, Tokyo, Japan
e-mail: takaoka@bus.seikei.ac.jp

S. Takaoka (ed.), *Environmental Technology Innovation and ESG Investment*,
https://doi.org/10.1007/978-981-99-9768-8_2

Varma (2014) document that the ESG equity funds perform relatively better than matched conventional mutual funds during market crisis periods. Correspondingly, Lins et al. (2017) demonstrate that US firms with higher CSR profiles attain higher stock returns during financial crises. Following these studies, Rjiba et al. (2020) unveil the efficacy of social capital from CSR activities in mitigating negative financial shocks in times of economic uncertainty, suggesting the increased value of CSR in turmoil periods.

Also, recent studies on ESG investing provide extensive evidence to recognize the importance of ESG engagement and ESG-related risk in asset prices, returns, and portfolio choices. Several studies empirically analyze this issue in the response of stock prices to the ESG-related risk, focusing on "sin" stocks (alcohol, tobacco, and gaming). For example, Hong and Kacperczyk (2009) study the stock prices and returns of sin stocks and find that sin stocks receive less coverage from analysts and have higher returns than otherwise comparable stocks. Similarly, Borgers et al. (2015) show the positive relation between mutual fund returns and sin stock exposure using the performance of US equity mutual funds between 2004 and 2012. Furthermore, a theoretical model in Colonnello et al. (2019) introduces an ethical preference-based model to study the sin-stock anomaly and discloses the non-pecuniary factors in the formation of investment decisions and asset prices.

Another strand of literature discusses the various aspects of the risk related to ESG investments. For example, Gibson Brandon and Krüger (2018) measure the portfolio-level environmental and social characteristics of institutional investors and show that the environmental and social portfolio policies can reduce the portfolio risk. Similarly, Fan and Michalski (2020) analyze the Australian stock market, demonstrating that portfolios with reduced risk can be constructed by considering ESG scores. Suto and Takehara (2020) also report that the CSR intensity stabilizes stock returns for high-CSR firms in the long run and moderates management disclosure bias in the short run based on the Japanese stock market. Moreover, Dunbar et al. (2020) find that CSR activities can lead to greater risk reduction for firms with governance characteristics indicating stronger information intensity/transparency and corporate social performance alignment. On the other hand, Hong and Kostovetsky (2012) reveal a connection between political value/bias and SRI fund management that explicit SRI funds are more likely to be managed by Democratic managers, highlighting a possible political bias in ESG investments. Additionally, Dunbar et al. (2021) provide strong evidence that as a firm's CSR status improves, increasing its risk-taking capacity, the firm responds by adjusting compensation contracts to increase CEO risk-taking incentives.

As can be seen, a growing number of studies document diverse pieces of evidence on the relationship between the asset prices and the firm's ESG performance. However, several research questions remain. The first is whether ESG performance is reflected in the pricing of bonds, which are less affected by growth options than stocks. Second, to what extent does each ESG issue affect corporate bond pricing through a firm's risk component? The third is whether the impact of ESG performance on asset pricing is constant across a firm's credit quality and over time. The primary objective of this study is to engage with these questions to make important contribution to the current literature.

An investigation of these questions necessitates the firm-level corporate bond credit spreads. Thus, our first contribution is to construct the firm-level corporate bond credit spreads and explore the impacts of a firm's ESG performance on corporate bond credit spreads in Japan. The corporate bond credit spread is considered to reflect the default risk of the corporate bond issuing firms; Longstaff et al. (2005) find that the majority of credit spreads are due to default risk. In this study, we construct firm credit spreads based on the "bottom-up" approach according to Gilchrist et al. (2009) and Gilchrist and Zakrajšek (2012). This method makes our firm-level credit spread data less contaminated by a small number of issuers with large outstanding corporate bonds compared to the individual bond issue level data. Consequently, this allows us to directly quantify the impact of a firm's ESG performance on its credit spreads to examine whether the market evaluates the risk of firms that differ in the sustainability associated with their ESG activities. There are several recent empirical studies on firms' ESG performances and individual corporate bond pricing, e.g., Stellner et al. (2015) on Eurozone corporate bonds and Jang et al. (2020) on ESG scores and bond returns in Korea. Our direct assessment reveals that ESG performance significantly reduces the corporate credit spreads, particularly for firms with the lower credit rating categories. Given that the engagement on ESG issues possibly enhances sustainability and decreases a firm's downside risk, as shown by Hoepner et al. (2020) using firms' stock return, it is quite sensible that lowly-rated issuing firms benefit more from the engagement on ESG issues.

Our second contribution is to investigate whether the impacts of ESG scores on corporate credit spreads are constant over time. Over the last decade or so, ESG investing developed considerably all over the world. Japan is not an exception. Particularly, ESG issues have become critical criteria for investment decisions in Japan since Japan's Government Pension Investment Fund (GPIF), the world's largest pension fund, became a signatory to the United Nation's Principles for Responsible Investment (PRI) on September 16, 2015. In addition, OECD (2020) documents the strong growth potential of Japan's sustainable investing (third largest center behind the EU and US) notwithstanding comparatively modest assets under management of approximately USD 2 trillion according to OECD (2020). As it took a longer time in the Japanese market than in the EU or US market before ESG investing sank in, the assumption relating to the constant impacts of ESG performance during our sample period might be unreasonable.[1] Therefore, it is instructive to examine possible increasing impacts of ESG performance on corporate credit spreads as the develop-

[1] It has also been motivating research with respect to environmental innovation, such as Acemoglu et al. (2018) who develop a microeconomic model of the transition to clean technology and find that both carbon taxes and research subsidies encourage production and innovation in clean technologies. In ESG investing, the research on green assets is enhanced; Pastor et al. (2020) theoretically model ESG criteria and find that investors enjoy holding green assets that hedge climate risk, resulting in having low expected returns; Krueger et al. (2020) explore the climate risk perceptions among institutional investors and their survey's findings indicate that institutional investors believe that equity valuations do not fully reflect the risks from climate change and consider climate risks as

ment of ESG investing. Specifically, we consider the recent upward momentum of ESG investing in the empirical analysis by employing the number of signatories to the PRI as a proxy for recognition of the importance of ESG investing globally. The findings indicate that the negative impacts of ESG scores on credit spreads have been increasing with the development of ESG investments. This result is independent of the sustainability measures and bond credit rating groups. However, our results also demonstrate that the increasing rates of the negative impacts for the lowly-rated firm group are much larger than those for the highly-rated firm group.

Our final contribution is to estimate the differential impacts of ESG categories on the corporate credit spreads, offering possibilities for a better understanding of the individual risk element of corporate ESG strategies in Japan. For the US, Bouslah et al. (2013) suggest positive/negative impacts of the individual dimensions of social performance on firm risk using the equity data. Our study contributes to the previous literature on the links between ESG engagements and corporate bond credit spreads by including the findings from the Japanese market. While our results show the lowering effects of ESG scores on corporate credit spreads, the significance and the magnitude of reduction in corporate spreads depend on the credit quality of issuing firms regardless of the ESG category scores. In addition, our results indicate that the resource use in the environment pillar, human right in the social pillar, and management categories in the governance pillar are the most influential in lowering the credit spreads.

Our main findings that corporate ESG performance is a significant determinant of corporate bond credit spreads also add to the literature on the determinants of corporate bond credit spreads. Our method to construct the firm-level credit spreads builds on Gilchrist and Zakrajšek (2012), who propose the "bottom-up" approach, and the results indicate that better ESG performance tends to lower credit spreads, even after controlling the issuing firm's financial health, credit rating, and three macroeconomic fundamental risk dimensions documented by Wu and Zhang (2008). Moreover, this result appears to be stronger for lowly-rated firms. To check the robustness of our results, we consider the potential endogeneity concern. Specifically, we address endogeneity concerns that could be due, for example, to the confounding factors that firms could achieve better ESG performance based on *ex ante* knowledge about risk surrounding. That could also affect the corporate default probability and hence corporate credit spreads. The instrumental variable (IV) results show that corporate ESG performance remains a significant factor for corporate bond credit spreads. This could be because the corporate bond credit spread in the secondary market is inherently forward-looking, see, e.g., Stock and Watson (2003), Gilchrist and Zakrajšek (2012), Faust et al. (2013), and Favara et al. (2016); in this sense, the reverse causality between credit spreads and ESG scores seems unlikely to be present, and we could reasonably overlook this issue. Our results of the stronger impacts of ESG scores on the credit scores for the lowly-rated firms further support this view.

---

important investment risks; while Baker et al. (2018) and Wang et al. (2020) estimate the green bond issuance premium in the US and China, respectively.

The remainder of this chapter is organized as follows: in Sect. 2, we describe the empirical strategy, construction of firm-level credit spread data and sample for our dataset, specifications to be estimated, and provide summary statistics. In Sect. 3, we present the main results, robustness check by employing the IV approach based on the two-stage least squares (2SLS), and results by a firm's credit quality. We investigate the impacts of ESG performance on corporate credit spreads across a firm's credit quality and over time in Sect. 4. The conclusions are presented in the final section.

2 Empirical Strategy

We investigate the relationship between a company's ESG performance and its credit spread in Japan. In response to the society's increasing demand for pro-social behavior, firms voluntarily provide relevant information to stakeholders. However, this type of information published by the firm may not be credible in nature, see Tirole (2017). Hence, we use the sustainability metrics at the firm-level provided by the ESG ratings provider and observable to the investor. Notwithstanding the shortcomings already reported by Boffo and Patalano (2020) regarding the strong variation of ESG ratings among providers owing to the different frameworks, measures, and data use, the growing use of ESG scores as a benchmark for ESG investing indicates that they provide useful reference points.

To address the research question relating to whether a firm's pro-social behavior decreases the perception of its risk as measured by corporate bond credit spreads, we construct the individual issuer's credit spreads in the following subsection. Thereafter, we discuss the empirical specification controls for the firm's financial and macroeconomic factors.

2.1 Data and Sample

We use a comprehensive dataset of individual corporate bond prices obtained from the Japan Standard Bond Price database, which includes such information as the interest rates, coupon rates, redemption dates, and issue dates of public and private offerings of domestic bonds, foreign bonds, and Eurobonds. This data source provides the most extensive coverage of secondary market prices of corporate bonds publicly issued in the Japanese market. To construct the individual firm's credit spreads, we limit our sample to only straight corporate bonds that are publicly issued in Japan by Japanese corporations. We exclude subordinated corporate bonds and Fiscal Investment and Loan Program agency bonds that are guaranteed by the central government. To ensure that we measure the borrowing costs of firms at the same point in their capital structures, we limit the sample to only senior issues with fixed coupon schedules, following prior studies. The original yield data have a daily frequency, and we use the last observed yield data in December to construct a dataset of year-end compound yields for individual corporate bond issues to match the ESG annual data.[2]

We use these data and those on the government bond zero curve to calculate the credit spread. The government bond yield data are obtained from Thomson Reuters Eikon, which collects market data on Japanese government bonds from Tradeweb and calculates the zero curve. Thomson Reuters Eikon offers government bond zero curve data with different maturities, ranging from one month to forty years. If the government bond zero curve is missing for a particular corporate bond maturity, it is filled via cubic spline interpolation.

We employ the "bottom-up" approach proposed by Gilchrist et al. (2009) and Gilchrist and Zakrajšek (2012) to construct the firm-level credit spread index. With individual corporate and government bond data, credit spreads are calculated as differences between corporate and government bond yields of the same maturity. Thus, we calculate credit spreads using corporate and government bond yields with exactly the same maturity. Thereafter, for the estimation, we obtain the year-end credit spreads of outstanding corporate bonds traded in the secondary market between 2007 and 2018. Our estimation sample of credit spreads is limited to corporate bonds with fixed coupon schedules and bullet bonds with no embedded options.

Specifically, the credit spread for corporate bond k with maturity m issued by firm i at time t is given by:

$$S_{imt}[k] = y_{imt}[k] - y^f_{mt}[k],$$

and $y_{imt}[k]$ is the yield of corporate bond k with maturity m at year t, while $y^f_{mt}[k]$ is the corresponding government bond yield of the thereafter same maturity at time t.

Given these credit spreads, we calculate the individual firm's credit spreads for bonds from the same firm as:

$$cs_{it} = \frac{1}{N_{it}} \sum_k S_{it}[k],$$

where N_{it} is the number of observations in year t of corporate bonds issued by firm i. That is, an individual firm i's credit spread in a given year is the arithmetic average of the firm's year-end credit spreads for its outstanding bonds.

We eliminate extreme observations including bond and month observations with credit spreads greater than 2,000 basis points following previous studies, such as that of Gilchrist and Zakrajšek (2012). As a lower bound, we eliminate observations with credit spreads below zero basis points to avoid including negative credit spreads which are economically nonsensical.

For the company's corporate responsibility commitments, we use four ESG scores provided by the Refinitiv (Thomson Reuters)—one of the largest ESG information providers—including MSCI, Sustainalytics, Bloomberg, and RobecoSAM Boffo and Patalano (2020) and have been employed in academic research, for example

[2] Because of this treatment, if a firm does not have any observed yield data in December, the firm is dropped from our dataset.

Table 1 Correlations of ESG score variables

	ESG score	Environmental	Social	Governance
ESG Score	1			
Environmental	0.723***	1		
Social	0.890***	0.508***	1	
Governance	0.844***	0.392***	0.662***	1

*$p < 0.05$, **$p < 0.01$, ***$p < 0.001$

Notes The table presents the correlations of the company's ESG performance: *ESG score*, *Environmental*, *Social*, and *Governance* scores

Stellner et al. (2015). The Refinitiv ESG scores are based on more than 500 different ESG metrics and simple to understand percentile rank scores benchmarked against TRBC Industry Group for all Environmental and Social categories, and against the Country for all Governance categories.[3] That is, these ESG scores control industry features. We use scores related to 10 main important categories: emission, innovation, resource use, CSR strategy, management, shareholders, community, human rights, product responsibility, and workforce. Of the 10 main categories, emission, innovation, and resource use are bunched into environmental score, while CSR strategy, management, and shareholders (community, human rights, product responsibility, and workforce) are rolled up into governance (social) score. We collect these ESG scores of Japanese listed firms from Datastream: ESG score and its three pillar scores, i.e., environmental, social, and governance scores, and 10 categorie scores.

According to the Refinitiv (Thomson Reuters) ESG scoring methodology, which produces a score between 0 and 100, the ESG score measures a company's ESG performance based on verifiable reported data in the public domain. Hence, we use this ESG score as a variable for the company's ESG performance. We also use three pillar scores, environmental, social, and governance scores, as variables for the company's performance in each important area. While we use four ESG scores in our estimation, Table 1 shows that these scores are highly correlated among themselves. That is, firms that receive a high score in one of the four variables tend to also receive high scores in the other variables. Hence, we do not use all four variables in the estimation simultaneously, but use each variable by itself.

We match the credit spread data and ESG scores with the firm's dataset, which includes credit rating and financial indicators, to control the firm's financial health and credit quality. Following previous studies, e.g., Stellner et al. (2015), financial indicators include firm's total revenue, earnings before interest and taxes (EBIT) margin (EBIT/total revenue), debt/capital, capital expenditure (CapEx)/total revenue, return on invested capital (ROIC), and equity volatility. Furthermore, the issuer's credit rating information is used to control the credit quality of the issuer. The firm's information is also taken from the Thomson Reuters database and is as of immediately prior to the year-end credit spread point.

[3] The details of the data process, global coverage, scores structure, and calculation methodology are explained in "Environmental, Social and Governance (ESG) scores from Refinitiv February 2021".

Finally, we incorporate three macroeconomic factors that Wu and Zhang (2008) identify three fundamental risk dimensions underlying an economy: inflation, real output growth, and financial market volatility. The growth rate (year-on-year) of the consumer price index (CPI) is used as an inflation factor. These data are obtained from the Statistics Bureau of Japan. As a real output growth variable, we use the real gross domestic product (GDP) growth (year-on-year) published by the Cabinet Office, Government of Japan. Lastly, we include the percent change in Nikkei Volatility Index (year-on-year) as a measure of the financial market volatility to capture the compound effect of business risk throughout the economy and financial leverage following Wu and Zhang (2008). This factor is considered to affect the pricing of corporate bond, as in Merton (1974).

The final sample is the unbalanced panel data that consist of 245 firms. The sample period is from 2007 to 2018.

2.2 Empirical Specification

Do well-performed ESG activities help hedge against ESG risks and lower a company's default risk? To address this question, we examine whether and how a company's ESG performances influence its credit spread, i.e., the cost of fundraising, after controlling for other characteristics of the credit spread determinants. To capture this effect, we estimate the following model:

$$Credit\ spread_{it} = \alpha_i + \delta ESG\ score_{it} + \gamma Controls_{it} + \beta Macro_t + \epsilon_{it} \quad (1)$$

where the dependent variable throughout our analysis is the year-end credit spread in basis points of a company i at time t. Using the year-end credit spreads minimizes the simultanity issues, making many of the explanatory variables predetermined. The explanatory variable of interest is the company's ESG performance measured in terms of the (i) ESG, (ii) environmental, (iii) social, and (iv) governance scores of company i at time t. Depending on the specification, we use one of the four ESG scores at a time due to their high correlation.

We include control variables, specific to company i, commonly used in the literature on credit spread determinants. These are credit rating and financial indicators: issuer's credit rating, logarithm of total revenue, EBIT margin (EBIT/total revenue), debt/capital, CapEx/total revenue, ROIC, and equity volatility. Based on a long strand of literature on the bond credit spread, we include a control for credit rating, as it directly affects bond credit spreads. For example, Ederington et al. (1987) and other subsequent papers show that credit ratings explain cross-sectional differences in bond credit spreads even after controlling for firm and issue characteristics, with a clear negative relation between changes in a bond's rating and changes in its credit spread. Therefore, we use the credit rating dummies to control the differences in adition to financial indicators. We also include a set of three macroeconomic variables at time t to capture the macroeconomic fluctuations that affect the movement of the credit spreads: the (year-on-year) growth rates of CPI and GDP, as well as the Nikkei Volatility Index. These are time series variables that are not specific to the company. Moreover, the model specification contains firm-fixed effects, α_i.[4]

The coefficient of interest is δ. The ESG scores take values between 0 and 100, meaning that the higher the better. While we use four different ESG scores as the explanatory variable, it holds in all four scores that the higher the better. If we find that δ is statistically significant and negative, then the ESG performance of a company is an important driver of credit spreads as well as beneficial to lowering the company's financing cost. We do not necessarily assume that each ESG factor, "E," "S," or "G" has a homogeneous impact on credit spreads. Their impacts or relevance to the economy may change over time during the sample period. We will consider the heterogeneity in impacts following the main results.

In specification (1), we assume that the ESG performance has a constant impact over time. This implies that the recent expansion of ESG investing is ignored in estimating the impacts. We extend the basic model to explore whether the impact of ESG scores on corporate credit spreads reflects the global trend toward facilitating ESG investment. Consequently, we modify (1) as follows:

$$\begin{aligned} Credit\ spread_{it} &= \alpha_i + \delta_1 ESG\ score_{it} + \delta_2 PRI_t ESG\ score_{it} + \gamma Controls_{it} \\ &\quad + \beta Macro_t + \epsilon_{it}. \end{aligned} \tag{2}$$

In addition to the inclusion of $ESG\ score_{it}$, we add an interaction term, $PRI_t ESG\ score_{it}$, between the number of signatories to the PRI published by the PRI and an ESG score to capture a global trend of sustainable finance. Since PRI_t can be a proxy for a global trend toward expanding sustainable finance, the interaction term allows for a differential effect on each ESG score on which the investor places emphasis during our sample period.[5]

2.3 Summary Statistics

The summary statistics for firm-specific variables to be used in the analysis are reported in Table 2, which decomposes the variables into between and within outputs. Our dataset is the unbalanced panel data from 2007 to 2018. The overall and within outputs are calculated over 2,353 firm-years of data. The rows labeled "overall" show the summary statistics calculated for the entire dataset; the "between" is calculated

[4] We have also tried to include the short-term Japanese government bond yield and the time-fixed effects to take the possible effect of monetary easing policy, they are not statistically significant for many cases. Therefore, we decided not to include them.

[5] Note that the coefficients of variation of PRI and ESG are 0.48 and 0.45, respectively, indicating that neither variables are a dominant factor of the interaction. We conduct a robustness check using an alternative proxy, e.g., a dummy for the period after GPIF becomes a signatory to the PRI, and confirm that the results are qualitatively similar. The results are not reported to conserve space.

over 245 firms (firm-level means). The average number of years a firm is observed in our data is approximately 10. The rows labeled "within" provide the information within each firm. The within output refers to the deviation from each firm's average, thus some of these deviations are naturally negative.[6]

As explained in Sect. 2.1, we eliminate extreme observations such that bond and month observations with credit spreads greater than 2,000 basis points or below zero basis points to avoid including negative credit spreads. We see that the average credit spreads for each firm vary between 15.2 and 1040.4. The figures within this range show that some firms significantly deviate from their average. The firm credit spread indicators have sufficient variation and reflect fluctuation over time because our sample period includes the global financial crisis period.

Note that the mean ESG score is 47.8. Similarly, the mean environmental and governance scores are 51.5 and 52.1, respectively. These scores take values between 0 and 100, thus our sample mean suggests that our dataset is not biased toward high- or low-performance firm groups. The mean social score is 40.3, which is slightly lower than that of the other scores. The "between" minimum and maximum values indicate that the firm-level means for the social score are not biased toward the low-performance groups.

In addition to the financial indicators in Table 2, the credit rating information is used in the estimation. The rating categories in the estimation sample range from AAA (approximately 1%) to CCC (approximately 0.2%). The average rating of the sample firms is the A rating category (approximately 59%).

3 Results

3.1 Benchmark Results

In this subsection, we report our benchmark results based on Eq. (1). One of the main contributions of this study is to examine whether and how a company's ESG performances influence its credit spreads, i.e., the cost of fundraising, after controlling for other characteristics of the credit spread determinants. Another contribution of our study is to separately investigate the impacts of ESG components on corporate spreads for the Japanese corporate bond market.

To measure the impacts of firm's ESG performance on corporate spreads, we estimate Eq. (1) via the panel fixed effects ordinary least squares (OLS) using the clustered standard errors by firms. We present the results for four sets of regressions. Each set uses a different sustainability measurement variable: ESG, environmental, social, or governance score. The estimation results are reported in Table 3. As evident in column (1) of Table 3, the coefficient of the ESG score, which is our main interest, is significantly negative, with an estimate of −0.65. This indicates that if the firm's

[6] The definition of "within" here is $x_{it} - \bar{x_i} + \bar{\bar{x}}$. The global mean $\bar{\bar{x}}$ is added back in so that the results are comparable.

Table 2 Descriptive statistics

		Mean	Std. dev.	Min	Max	N/n/$\bar{T}$
Credit spread (bp)	Overall	46.1	91.7	7.1	1864.1	2353
	Between		75.8	15.2	1040.4	245
	Within		65.5	−793.3	1083.8	10
ESG score	Overall	47.8	20.0	2.2	89.9	2353
	Between		18.9	3.8	82.6	245
	Within		7.7	0.5	87.2	10
Environmental score	Overall	51.5	23.7	2.1	98.4	2353
	Between		21.1	6.7	95.7	245
	Within		11.8	−5.6	90.4	10
Governance score	Overall	52.1	27.2	0	97.4	2353
	Between		25.6	0	92.9	245
	Within		10.7	−26.2	115.1	10
Social score	Overall	40.3	22.4	0.26	93.9	2353
	Between		20.5	2.0	85.6	245
	Within		10.2	−6.0	86.4	10
Revenues (JPYbn)	Overall	1713.5	2525.5	15	29000	2353
	Between		2359.8	32.1	24000	245
	Within		493.5	−3286.5	6713.5	10
EBIT margin	Overall	0.08	0.09	−1.0	0.65	2353
	Between		0.08	−0.03	0.61	245
	Within		0.06	−0.89	0.57	10
Debt/capital	Overall	0.55	0.42	0	12.0	2353
	Between		0.34	0.002	2.31	245
	Within		0.26	−1.39	10.2	10
Capex/revenue	Overall		0.08	0	1	2353
	Between		0.07	0.001	0.67	245
	Within		0.03	−0.18	0.56	10
ROIC	Overall	4.2	4.5	−34.7	25.8	2353
	Between		2.9	−7.1	19.1	245
	Within		3.7	−27.4	21.9	10
Equity volatility	Overall	26.4	6.9	10.8	55.0	2353
	Between		6.3	13.4	49.5	245
	Within		3.1	11.7	41.6	10

Notes The table presents the summary statistics for the unbalanced panel data from 2007 to 2018. N, n, and $\bar{T}$ refer to the observations with firm-year data, the number of firms, and the average number of years per issuing firm, respectively

ESG score increases by 1 point, the credit spread of the firm tends to decrease by 0.65 basis points. This means that the ESG score could affect credit spread by 65 basis points at the maximum, as the ESG scores take values between 0 and 100. Given the extremely low interest rate environments in Japan over the last two decades or thereabouts, this can be considered a relatively significant impact.

Many control variables are significant with most of them showing expected relationships. For example, the credit rating dummies indicate that credit spreads approximately increase monotonically as the credit rating worsens. The only exception is the relation between AAA and AA ratings, where the results indicate that both ratings essentially have the same credit spreads on average. This is because Japanese corporate bonds with AA ratings are considered to have almost no default risk with no significant difference from those with AAA ratings. The logarithm of total revenue is significantly positive, which is highly contrary to the results of Stellner et al. (2015), showing an interesting difference between Japanese and European corporate bond markets. One possible reason for the difference is that in Japan, firms with larger revenues tend to issue more corporate bonds, thereby paying more premia. Another significant firm variable is the ROIC with a negative sign, which is consistent with Stellner et al. (2015), reflecting lower default risk. All macroeconomic control variables are significant with expected signs. Specifically, GDP growth rates have negative signs, suggesting that good economic conditions generally lower credit spreads. Similarly, inflation tends to decrease credit spreads, as higher inflation is associated with the better economic condition for our sample period in Japan. Finally, stock price volatility changes have positive signs because higher uncertainty in the stock market generally reduces risk appetite in financial markets.

To investigate the impact of ESG pillars on corporate spreads separately, we re-estimate Eq. (1) using the score of each pillar rather than the ESG score.[7] The estimation results are summarized in the last three columns of Table 3, showing a clear difference between the environmental pillar and the other two pillars. While the environmental score shows no significant impact on credit spreads, the social and governance scores have significantly negative effects on credit spreads. In other words, firms with higher social and governance scores can enjoy lower credit spreads, but firms cannot benefit from the higher environmental score. Against the backdrop of the global trend for tackling climate change, the insignificant impact of the environmental score on credit spreads seems counterintuitive. Notably, Japanese companies own more environment-related technologies than those in other countries; Haščič and Migotto (2015) shows that Japan has the highest ratio of the world's high-value inventions among foremost inventor countries globally in environment-related technologies between 2009 and 2011. Judging from the fact that Japan is at least one of the top performers in environmental-related technologies in Haščič and Migotto (2015), Japanese companies are considered sensitive to environmental issues. But at the same time, this implies that those companies with higher environmental scores might overinvest in environmental issues, possibly offsetting the lowering impact of

[7] The high correlation among these scores can cause the multicollinearity problem; thus, we conduct estimations separately throughout this study.

Table 3 Credit spreads and sustainability measures: panel OLS results

	(1)	(2)	(3)	(4)
	ESG score	Environmental score	Social score	Governance score
Sustainability measurement	−0.65[b] (0.279)	−0.11 (0.124)	−0.39[b] (0.172)	−0.45[b] (0.189)
AAA rating	−1063.88[a] (101.768)	−1063.89[a] (101.868)	−1062.93[a] (102.112)	−1069.27[a] (102.600)
AA rating	−1065.40[a] (101.266)	−1063.53[a] (101.124)	−1063.68[a] (101.320)	−1070.40[a] (102.088)
A rating	−1050.07[a] (100.624)	−1048.13[a] (100.458)	−1048.08[a] (100.666)	−1054.76[a] (101.370)
BBB rating	−1010.59[a] (96.742)	−1007.96[a] (96.498)	−1008.39[a] (96.838)	−1016.31[a] (97.358)
BB rating	−660.39[a] (128.155)	−664.31[a] (126.618)	−660.46[a] (129.647)	−668.76[a] (126.833)
B rating	−553.36[a] (123.684)	−557.09[a] (124.189)	−551.21[a] (125.117)	−560.73[a] (123.812)
ln(Revenue)	49.32[c] (26.067)	45.64[c] (25.698)	47.76[c] (25.919)	49.79[c] (26.038)
EBIT margin	−71.81 (96.934)	−73.62 (96.879)	−71.50 (97.302)	−74.88 (97.303)
Debt/capital	−1.36 (10.160)	−0.57 (10.678)	−1.25 (10.267)	−1.11 (10.243)
Capex/revenue	113.49 (69.231)	111.94 (68.432)	108.74 (69.607)	113.62 (71.174)
ROIC	−2.54[c] (1.388)	−2.53[c] (1.400)	−2.50[c] (1.382)	−2.56[c] (1.392)
Price volatility	0.33 (0.823)	0.39 (0.819)	0.27 (0.837)	0.35 (0.812)
Δ GDP	−3.62[a] (0.573)	−3.74[a] (0.568)	−3.70[a] (0.571)	−3.58[a] (0.576)
Δ CPI	−7.08[a] (2.502)	−7.35[a] (2.530)	−7.14[a] (2.512)	−7.02[a] (2.487)
Δ NVIX	0.28[a] (0.029)	0.30[a] (0.031)	0.29[a] (0.030)	0.28[a] (0.028)
Firm fixed effects	Yes	Yes	Yes	Yes
Observations	2353	2353	2353	2353
Adjusted R^2	0.60	0.60	0.60	0.60

Notes The table presents the estimation results of Eq. (1),
$Credit\ spread_{it} = \alpha_i + \delta ESG\ score_{it} + \gamma Controls_{it} + \beta Macro_t + \epsilon_{it}$,
based on sustainability measurements (1) ESG, (2) Environmental, (3) Governance, and (4) Social scores of issuing firms, their financial indicators, and macroeconomic controls. Baseline rating category is below CCC. Standard errors (SE) clustered at the firm level in parenthesis. [a] significant at 1%, [b] significant at 5%, [c] significant at 10%

higher environmental scores on credit spreads. In addition, it is ambiguous whether the estimated impact of the environmental score incorporates the recent social preference to aggressively tackle the environmental issue. In other words, the results of this section could underestimate the impact of ESG scores, particularly for the environmental score, due to the ignorance of the recent increasing attention on ESG issues, including the carbon efficiency and climate change risk. We will investigate this aspect in the next section.

3.2 Instruments and 2SLS

We so far show the empirical results that the better ESG performance reduces the corporate credit spreads. However, the causal relationship between credit spreads and ESG performance is not addressed. With regard to the reverse causality between credit spread and ESG performance, we are less concerned about this issue because we use the end-of-year corporate credit spreads, making the most of explanatory variables predetermined, and corporate bond credit spreads in the secondary market are inherently forward-looking, see, e.g., Stock and Watson (2003), Gilchrist and Zakrajšek (2012), Faust et al. (2013), and Favara et al. (2016). It seems unlikely that the past corporate ESG activities are determined by corporate credit spread, a forward-looking variable. Therefore, it is not unreasonable to assume no reverse causality.

With regard to the omitted variables problem, we include control variables as many as Stellner et al. (2015) and three macroeconomic fundamental risk dimensions in Wu and Zhang (2008). Hence, it is also not unreasonable to assume that our principal results are not driven by omitted variables about economic conditions or firm-specific factors.

To rule out endogeneity issues, we include the independent variables prior to the year-end credit spread point. In this subsection, we further address any remaining endogeneity concerns. To alleviate any possible endogeneity concern about the causal impact of ESG performance on credit spreads, we now employ an IV approach based on the 2SLS. We need variables that have a significant correlation with company ESG performance but do not affect company credit spreads. Literature on firm ESG performance and credit risk enables us to identify a possible instrument for corporate ESG performance: the average company score for each sustainability measurement of all other companies in the same sector and the same year Jiraporn et al. (2014). The idea is that the credit spreads may be related to firm-level ESG performance, however, it is less likely to the sector-level ESG performance. Taking into account that there are many firms in a sector, changes in ESG performance at the sector-level are more likely exogenous. The results of the first stage regression, though not reported to save space, show that an instrument has significant explanatory power as indicated by its positive and highly significant coefficient.

Table 4 reports the estimation results of Eq. (1) from the IV approach based on 2SLS which includes each sustainability measurement instrumented with its corresponding average sustainability measurement of all other companies in the same sector and in the same year. The 2SLS results are restricted to those on the second stage to save space.[8] The relationship between ESG performance and credit spreads remains unchanged with an instrument, mitigating the concerns that our results are driven by the endogeneity.

Note that the test for exogeneity of the environmental score as an ESG measure in column (2) of Table 4 fails to reject the null hypothesis that the environmental score is exogenous. The environmental score coefficient in our main results in Table 3 is not significant, and it remains insignificant in Table 4. Hence, our main results remain qualitatively the same. The ESG pillar scores in columns (1)–(4) of Table 4 bear negative coefficients. Each of them is statistically significant in all specifications, except for column (2), which is also insignificant in Table 3. Overall, the corresponding effect is higher, and the IV results are stronger in terms of the magnitude of the estimated effects relative to the OLS results, but the statistical significance is similar. In line with Stellner et al. (2015), we confirm our results with another instrument variable that is the average company score for each sustainability measurement of all other companies in the same year, assuming that the country-level ESG performance in the same year is more likely to exogenous. The results are not reported, however, they are qualitatively similar. The results demonstrate that the endogeneity issue is not a serious concern, as we predicted. Therefore, we will use the OLS for the rest of the analysis.

3.3 Credit Quality

The previous subsections provide clear evidence of a negative relationship between ESG scores and credit spreads. That is, the firm that attains a better ESG performance can enjoy a lower financing cost. Additional analysis indicates that the social and governance scores play a more important role in this negative relationship than the environmental score. One of the key assumptions for the analyses so far is that the effects of ESG scores are homogeneous across firms regardless of their credit quality. However, it could be possible that higher ESG scores can provide stronger signals for corporate bonds in lower credit rating categories. This is because one possible reason why higher ESG scores lower credit spreads is that the former is closely related to the firm's sustainability. If this is the case, it is reasonable that there is a negative relationship between ESG scores and the credit risk of firms. Consequently, high ESG scores could reduce firms' credit spreads. However, this also suggests that firms with little credit risk should not be considerably affected by ESG scores, making additional information on higher sustainability due to the higher ESG scores less informative. On the other hand, for those firms with lower credit ratings, higher ESG scores could have precious information on higher sustainability from the non-financial information perspective. In other words, only firms whose credit risk is

[8] The first stage results are available upon request.

Table 4 Credit spreads and sustainability measures: 2SLS results

	(1)	(2)	(3)	(4)
	ESG score	Environmental score	Social score	Governance score
Sustainability measurement	−1.82[a]	−2.28	−1.24[a]	−1.06[a]
	(0.592)	(1.927)	(0.419)	(0.381)
AAA rating	−520.38[a]	−524.16[a]	−519.64[a]	−514.76[a]
	(137.460)	(133.123)	(140.258)	(136.691)
AA rating	−525.71[a]	−525.46[a]	−523.22[a]	−518.33[a]
	(137.624)	(129.951)	(140.064)	(136.475)
A rating	−511.65[a]	−514.24[a]	−508.38[a]	−503.45[a]
	(139.289)	(131.568)	(141.613)	(138.156)
BBB rating	−470.41[a]	−466.16[a]	−466.67[a]	−464.39[a]
	(139.135)	(131.277)	(141.443)	(137.934)
ln(Revenue)	48.56[b]	40.28[c]	45.03[b]	47.79[b]
	(21.858)	(21.176)	(21.385)	(20.133)
EBIT margin	−15.99	−18.01	−14.41	−22.42
	(56.549)	(54.816)	(56.920)	(56.200)
Debt/capital	−0.63	−1.32	−0.05	0.36
	(8.127)	(8.453)	(8.104)	(8.113)
Capex/revenue	118.35[c]	151.49[b]	104.27	117.11
	(68.023)	(68.451)	(69.579)	(71.869)
ROIC	−2.68[b]	−2.76[b]	−2.58[b]	−2.72[b]
	(1.321)	(1.371)	(1.301)	(1.342)
Price volatility	0.44	0.66	0.24	0.53
	(0.824)	(0.866)	(0.885)	(0.796)
Δ GDP	−3.65[a]	−3.95[a]	−3.82[a]	−3.59[a]
	(0.623)	(0.667)	(0.616)	(0.639)
Δ CPI	−6.56[a]	−7.64[a]	−6.64[a]	−6.52[b]
	(2.513)	(2.846)	(2.522)	(2.578)
Δ NVIX	0.25[a]	0.29[a]	0.26[a]	0.25[a]
	(0.029)	(0.035)	(0.029)	(0.030)
Firm fixed effects	Yes	Yes	Yes	Yes
Observations	2347	2347	2347	2347
Kleibergen-Paap underid.	56.80	4.08	72.96	58.80
p-val	0.00	0.04	0.00	0.00
Kleibergen-Paap weak id.	96.54	4.20	135.95	81.80

Notes The table presents the estimation results of Eq. (1),
$Credit\ spread_{it} = \alpha_i + \delta ESG\ score_{it} + \gamma Controls_{it} + \beta Macro_t + \epsilon_{it}$,
based on 2SLS. Reported coefficients and standard errors are from second stage regressions from a 2SLS regression analysis of the influence of each sustainability measurement on corporate bond credit spreads which include the instrumented values of sustainability measurement as independent variable. Each sustainability measurement is instrumented with its corresponding average sustainability measurement of all other companies in the same sector and in the same year. Baseline rating category is below the BB-rated categories. SE clustered at the firm level in parenthesis. [a] significant at 1%, [b] significant at 5%, [c] significant at 10%

non-negligible can comparatively benefit from higher ESG scores. Therefore, in this subsection, we will relax the homogeneity assumption across credit quality to determine whether our results are robust for the assumption and provide more precise insights if some heterogeneity exists.

To examine the possible differences in the effects of ESG scores on credit spreads between low and high credit risk firms, we divide the sample based on the credit rating information. In Japan, firms with A rating or above are considered to have little default risk in general. Notably, firms with AAA and AA ratings have rarely failed over the last 20 years in Japan, and the default risk of A rating is generally considered to be less than 1%. However, the default risk of firms with BBB rating or below is typically regarded as non-negligible, although the defaults of BBB-rated firms are still rather seldomly observed in Japan, except in 2009 when two defaults of BBB-rated firms have been reported, according to the Moody's rating. Therefore, it is fair to say that there is little credit risk for the firms with A rating or above in Japan, but there exists some credit risk for firms with BBB rating or below. Given this observation, we split the sample into two groups depending on whether the firm's rating is A or above, or BBB or below, whereafter we re-estimate model (1) using each subsample.

Table 5 presents the estimation results for each subsample, and we can find noticeable differences between the two subsamples. Specifically, for the A-rated or above firm group, although the ESG score shows a significantly negative impact on credit spread, each pillar's score is insignificant. Moreover, the magnitude of the significant impact of the ESG score is estimated as −0.17 bps, which is less than one-third of that of the previous subsection. Similar tendencies can be observed in macroeconomic variables, meaning that the effects of the macroeconomic variables are significant but generally weaker for this group. These observations are consistent with our prediction that those variables implying lower credit risk have smaller effects on credit spreads for small credit risk firms.

Nonetheless, for the BBB-rated or below firm group, the ESG scores have a significantly negative impact on credit spreads with a much larger magnitude than that of the previous subsection and the A-rated or above firm group. For the BBB-rated or below firm group, if the ESG score increases by one point, the credit spread tends to be lower by 3.25 bps, which is approximately five times that presented in Table 3 and more than 20 times the impact compared to the A-rated or above firm group. Furthermore, for the BBB-rated or below firm group, the social and governance pillar scores show significantly negative effects on credit spreads with estimates of −2.59 and −2.63, respectively. This result is consistent with that of the previous subsection in terms of significance but also indicates an interesting difference in the magnitude. The magnitudes of the impacts of the macroeconomic variables also indicate the same tendencies. These results are reasonable, as those variables that can be a signal for the lower credit risk should have larger impacts on credit spreads for higher credit risk firms.

In sum, the results in this subsection clearly show the greater impacts of ESG scores on lowering credit spreads for lower graded firms. In other words, the information on higher ESG scores is more informative for those firms that are considered

Table 5 By credit rating levels

	High (above A rating)				Low (below BBB rating)			
	ESG score	Environmental score	Social score	Governance score	ESG score	Environmental score	Social score	Governance score
Sustainability measurement	-0.17^{c} (0.086)	−0.06 (0.052)	−0.09 (0.057)	−0.07 (0.062)	-3.25^{b} (1.324)	−0.57 (0.634)	-2.59^{b} (1.126)	-2.63^{b} (1.159)
AAA rating	−5.07 (4.775)	−5.49 (4.643)	−5.36 (5.372)	−5.37 (5.112)				
AA rating	-8.97^{a} (2.715)	-8.91^{a} (2.682)	-9.02^{a} (2.691)	-9.00^{a} (2.687)				
BBB rating					-294.09^{a} (30.764)	-274.49^{a} (29.664)	-274.14^{a} (28.810)	-296.35^{a} (32.558)
ln(Revenue)	4.13 (6.593)	3.04 (6.573)	3.68 (6.645)	3.70 (6.801)	175.02 (106.024)	183.34^{c} (105.532)	166.90 (107.306)	194.18* (105.807)
EBIT margin	38.21 (67.001)	37.85 (66.813)	38.18 (67.042)	37.44 (67.154)	−391.05 (411.465)	−358.42 (416.650)	−393.01 (404.242)	−385.53 (415.197)
Debt/capital	21.02^{b} (10.319)	22.04^{b} (10.108)	21.28^{b} (10.459)	21.61^{b} (10.243)	−12.59 (11.266)	−12.98 (11.665)	−12.57 (10.413)	−11.10 (10.966)
Capex/revenue	92.46 (60.610)	92.23 (60.386)	90.97 (60.832)	91.78 (60.723)	514.74^{b} (242.274)	600.16^{b} (248.722)	555.89^{b} (261.581)	510.46^{c} (256.804)
ROIC	-0.71^{c} (0.425)	−0.70 (0.424)	-0.70^{c} (0.424)	-0.71^{c} (0.423)	−5.15 (5.065)	−6.04 (5.331)	−5.02 (4.734)	−5.32 (5.149)
Price volatility	0.51^{b} (0.224)	0.51^{b} (0.224)	0.49^{b} (0.225)	0.51^{b} (0.224)	−6.50 (4.407)	−5.73 (4.408)	−7.48 (4.672)	−6.64 (4.347)
Δ GDP	-2.82^{a} (0.352)	-2.84^{a} (0.350)	-2.83^{a} (0.352)	-2.82^{a} (0.357)	-9.46^{a} (3.083)	-9.80^{a} (3.153)	-9.73^{a} (3.061)	-8.90^{a} (3.129)
Δ CPI	-2.95^{a} (0.364)	-3.01^{a} (0.365)	-2.98^{a} (0.357)	-2.97^{a} (0.359)	-31.74^{b} (12.280)	-30.54^{b} (12.451)	-30.38^{b} (12.482)	-30.11^{b} (12.190)
Δ NVIX	0.19^{a} (0.015)	0.20^{a} (0.015)	0.19^{a} (0.015)	0.19^{a} (0.015)	0.77^{a} (0.168)	0.78^{a} (0.191)	0.74^{a} (0.179)	0.71^{a} (0.175)
Firm fixed effects	Yes	Yes	Yes	Yes	Yes	Yes	Yes	Yes
Observations	2041	2041	2041	2041	312	312	312	312
Adjusted R^2	0.55	0.55	0.55	0.55	0.68	0.68	0.68	0.68

Notes The table shows OLS estimations of Eq. (1),

$$Credit\ spread_{it} = \alpha_i + \delta ESG\ score_{it} + \gamma Controls_{it} + \beta Macro_t + \epsilon_{it},$$

by issuer's credit rating levels. The first four columns present results using the firm-level credit spreads for highly-rated issuers, while the last four columns for lowly-rated issuers. SE clustered at the firm level in parenthesis. [a] significant at 1%, [b] significant at 5%, [c] significant at 10%

to have higher default risk from the financial information. The results also imply that the reverse causality from lower credit spreads to higher ESG scores is not an issue in our analysis. If it captures the reverse causality from credit spreads to ESG scores, the results in this subsection should be the opposite, as those firms with higher credit ratings should have more capability to have higher ESG scores. Thus, there should be a stronger relationship between credit spreads and ESG scores for the A-rated or above firms. However, the results in this subsection indicate that this is not the case, providing further evidence that the reverse causality is not an issue in the analysis of this study.

4 Global Trends of Responsible Investment

In this section, we study possible mechanisms through which ESG performance has an impact on credit spreads by exploring how the global trends of responsible investment affect credit spreads over time. Another key assumption for the analyses so far is that the effects of ESG performance are stable over time. However, the role of ESG performance can be more important in the market, as ESG investing develops in more recent years. Therefore, we will relax this homogeneity assumption across time to determine whether company ESG performance can affect corporate bond credit spreads more through the growing pressure from the investors who are concerned about the responsible investment.

4.1 Effects of PRI Signatories

Over the last decade, ESG investing has been attracting considerable attention. As a natural consequence, the level of ESG investment has grown significantly over the past 10 years. This suggests that investors have begun to pay more attention to the ESG performance of firms when they make investment decisions. One possible implication of this fact is that ESG scores might play a more important role in financial markets with the development of ESG investments. We focus on this channel, which gains little attention in the previous works. With a concrete indicator, the number of PRI signatories, we examine whether ESG scores should have larger impacts on credit spreads more recently under the growing pressure from such investors. Put differently, the increase in the number of PRI signatories should increase the impact of higher ESG performance on corporate sustainability, which should translate into lower credit risk, then lead to the reduction in credit spreads.

The goal of the analysis in this subsection is to examine whether the impact of ESG scores on credit spreads has been stronger with the development of ESG investments. Thus, we modify the benchmark regression model (1) to capture the possible time-varying effects of ESG scores, thereby reflecting the development of ESG investments. Specifically, our new regression model is given by Eq. (2) by adding an interaction term between the ESG score and a measure of the development of ESG investments evaluated by the number of PRI signatories. In this specification, the effects of the ESG score will change with the number of PRI signatories. More specifically, the impact can be calculated as: $\delta_1 + \delta_2 PRI_t$.

Table 6 reports the estimation results of Eq. 2 based on the full sample. An important result of this table is that, with this specification, the coefficient on the ESG measure is not significant anymore regardless of the ESG measures. Conversely, the coefficient on the interaction term is highly significant for all ESG measures, including the environmental score. This is a great contrast to the results of the previous section, where we could not find any significant evidence of a negative relationship between the environmental score and credit spreads. More importantly, this result indicates that the effects of ESG scores on credit spreads have been increasing with the development of ESG investments, as measured by the number of PRI signatories. For example, if the number of PRI signatories increases by 1, the negative impact of the ESG score on credit spreads increases by 0.0002. Given that the number of PRI signatories has exceeded 3000 in 2020, the total effects could be substantial. To elucidate this point clearly, we plot the evolution of the impact of ESG scores on credit spreads based on the estimation results of Table 6 in Panel (a) of Fig. 1. Apparently, the impacts of the ESG scores increase rather linearly with the development of ESG investments. As of 2020, the negative impacts range from 0.24 to 0.50 basis points, depending on the ESG measures.

To accommodate the possible difference in the effects of ESG scores between the credit ratings, we also estimate Eq. (2) using the subsamples, namely the A-rated or above, and BBB-rated or below firm groups. The estimation results are shown in Table 7. Evidently, although none of the coefficients of the ESG measure is significant, that of the interaction term is highly significant for all cases. These results are consistent with those of the previous section, but they also show a clear tendency that the magnitude of the coefficient on the interaction term is strikingly larger for the BBB-rated or below firm group. This result is similar to the finding of the previous sections, but the current result means that the increasing rates in the impacts of ESG scores for the BBB-rated or below firm group are considerably higher than those for the A-rated or above firm group. To see this graphically, Panels (b) and (c) of Fig. 1 plot the evolution of the impact of ESG scores on credit spreads based on the estimation results of Table 7. The graphs suggest that the negative impact of ESG scores increases rather linearly with the development of ESG investments for both groups, but the increasing rates for the BBB-rated or below group are much larger. Therefore, as of 2020, the negative impacts range from 0.17 to 0.23 basis points for the A-rated or above group, but the corresponding range is from 2.0 to 4.3 basis points for the BBB-rated or below group.

In sum, the results in this subsection are clear cut and consistent with the expected relationship that the negative impacts of ESG scores on credit spreads have been increasing with the development of ESG investments. This result is independent of the sustainability measures and bond credit rating groups. The results can be considered as another evidence that the endogeneity is not a serious issue in our analysis. Otherwise, the investors ESG awareness cannot strengthen the impact of

Table 6 Effects of signatory to the United Nation's Principles for Responsible Investment

	(1)	(2)	(3)	(4)
	ESG score	Environmental score	Social score	Governance score
Sustainability measurement	−0.24 (0.356)	0.16 (0.151)	−0.03 (0.227)	−0.22 (0.230)
Sustainability measurement× PRI	−0.0002[b] (0.00009)	−0.0003[a] (0.00008)	−0.0002[b] (0.00009)	−0.0001[b] (0.00006)
AAA rating	−1083.30[a] (104.392)	−1090.26[a] (104.909)	−1080.93[a] (105.396)	−1082.22[a] (104.311)
AA rating	−1080.42[a] (103.021)	−1086.23[a] (103.400)	−1077.53[a] (103.523)	−1079.67[a] (103.146)
A rating	−1061.02[a] (101.908)	−1065.76[a] (102.172)	−1058.86[a] (102.346)	−1060.71[a] (102.032)
BBB rating	−1021.00[a] (98.297)	−1025.99[a] (98.510)	−1018.31[a] (98.605)	−1021.60[a] (98.133)
BB rating	−663.26[a] (129.009)	−669.26[a] (128.269)	−662.65[a] (130.155)	−667.12[a] (128.222)
B rating	−550.62[a] (122.173)	−555.45[a] (121.804)	−549.50[a] (123.395)	−554.20[a] (122.918)
ln(Revenue)	55.25[b] (27.437)	54.76[b] (27.211)	53.49[c] (27.437)	54.88[b] (27.103)
EBIT margin	−70.38 (97.298)	−66.80 (97.649)	−71.93 (97.436)	−74.38 (97.309)
Debt/capital	−3.19 (9.109)	−3.49 (9.007)	−2.78 (9.381)	−2.65 (9.384)
Capex/revenue	109.91 (67.874)	103.76 (64.229)	109.13 (69.008)	110.83 (70.020)
ROIC	−2.51[c] (1.367)	−2.55[c] (1.378)	−2.47[c] (1.362)	−2.52[c] (1.370)
Price volatility	0.15 (0.861)	0.09 (0.862)	0.13 (0.873)	0.24 (0.847)
Δ GDP	−3.23[a] (0.602)	−3.14[a] (0.596)	−3.33[a] (0.604)	−3.27[a] (0.601)
Δ CPI	−5.99[a] (2.290)	−5.51[b] (2.233)	−6.27[a] (2.318)	−6.18[a] (2.368)
Δ NVIX	0.26[a] (0.029)	0.25[a] (0.028)	0.27[a] (0.029)	0.27[a] (0.029)
Firm fixed effects	Yes	Yes	Yes	Yes
Observations	2353	2353	2353	2353
Adjusted R^2	0.60	0.60	0.60	0.60

Notes The table presents the estimation results of Eq. (2),

$$Credit\ spread_{it} = \alpha_i + \delta_1 ESG\ score_{it} + \delta_2 PRI_t ESG\ score_{it} + \gamma Controls_{it} + \beta Macro_t + \epsilon_{it},$$

based on sustainability measurements (1) ESG, (2) Environmental, (3) Governance, and (4) Social scores of issuing firms, the interaction between sustainability measurement and the number of signatories to the PRI, their financial indicators, and macroeconomic controls. Baseline rating category is the below CCC-rated categories. SE clustered at the firm level in parenthesis. [a] significant at 1%, [b] significant at 5%, [c] significant at 10%

Table 7 By credit rating levels

	High (above A rating)				Low (below BBB rating)			
	ESG score	Environmental score	Social score	Governance score	ESG score	Environmental score	Social score	Governance score
Sustainability measurement	0.08 (0.139)	0.06 (0.062)	0.12 (0.111)	0.08 (0.086)	−1.62 (1.111)	1.24 (0.853)	0.22 (1.144)	−1.23 (1.139)
Sustainability measurement × PRI	−0.0001[a] (0.00004)	−0.0001[a] (0.00003)	−0.0001[a] (0.00004)	−0.0001[a] (0.00003)	−0.0017[a] (0.0005)	−0.0022[a] (0.0007)	−0.0019[b] (0.0008)	−0.0012[b] (0.0006)
AAA rating	−10.05 (7.792)	−9.34 (6.826)	−9.55 (7.892)	−10.06 (7.623)				
AA rating	−11.27[a] (3.034)	−11.07[a] (3.035)	−10.74[a] (2.941)	−11.19[a] (2.996)				
BBB rating					−337.00[a] (37.143)	−342.76[a] (39.586)	−326.44[a] (40.412)	−327.30[a] (35.487)
ln(Revenue)	8.00 (6.985)	7.43 (6.702)	7.33 (7.070)	7.78 (7.150)	166.63 (104.551)	174.22[c] (99.510)	167.90 (105.966)	180.48 (107.993)
EBIT margin	37.62 (67.523)	39.40 (67.515)	36.56 (67.319)	36.85 (67.484)	−412.16 (409.422)	−358.01 (413.652)	−399.38 (407.794)	−403.29 (409.293)
Debt/capital	16.47[c] (9.573)	16.08[c] (9.600)	17.67[c] (9.802)	17.30[c] (9.529)	−13.09 (8.469)	−15.54 (9.427)	−14.91[c] (8.679)	−12.02 (9.105)
Capex/revenue	92.89 (59.974)	91.84 (58.689)	93.70 (60.682)	92.19 (60.204)	367.85 (239.283)	351.66 (219.088)	415.96[c] (231.973)	401.58 (258.528)
ROIC	−0.70 (0.428)	−0.73[c] (0.428)	−0.68 (0.426)	−0.70 (0.426)	−3.83 (4.295)	−4.91 (4.660)	−4.42 (4.282)	−4.52 (4.588)
Price volatility	0.39[c] (0.219)	0.38[c] (0.227)	0.39[c] (0.217)	0.43[c] (0.221)	−8.79[c] (4.626)	−9.34[c] (4.894)	−8.94[c] (4.972)	−8.24[c] (4.731)
Δ GDP	−2.59[a] (0.330)	−2.60[a] (0.333)	−2.63[a] (0.329)	−2.61[a] (0.338)	−7.84[b] (3.132)	−7.27[b] (3.224)	−8.41[b] (3.133)	−7.84[b] (3.178)
Δ CPI	−2.40[a] (0.376)	−2.30[a] (0.390)	−2.56[a] (0.363)	−2.49[a] (0.390)	−24.46[c] (12.767)	−19.90 (11.983)	−23.26[c] (12.753)	−23.89[c] (13.449)
Δ NVIX	0.18[a] (0.013)	0.18[a] (0.013)	0.19[a] (0.014)	0.18[a] (0.013)	0.57[a] (0.181)	0.47[b] (0.206)	0.60[a] (0.189)	0.56[a] (0.202)
Firm fixed effects	Yes	Yes	Yes	Yes	Yes	Yes	Yes	Yes
Observations	2041	2041	2041	2041	312	312	312	312
Adjusted R^2	0.56	0.55	0.56	0.56	0.68	0.68	0.68	0.69

Notes: The table shows the estimation results of Eq. (2),

$$Credit\ spread_{it} = \alpha_i + \delta_1 ESG\ score_{it} + \delta_2 PRI_t ESG\ score_{it} + \gamma Controls_{it} + \beta Macro_t + \epsilon_{it},$$

based on sustainability measurements (1) ESG, (2) Environmental, (3) Governance, and (4) Social scores of issuing firms, the interaction between sustainability measurement and the number of signatories to the PRI, their financial indicators, and macroeconomic controls by issuer's credit rating levels. The first four columns present results using firm-level credit spreads for highly-rated issuers, while the last four columns show the results for lowly-rated issuers. SE clustered at the firm level in parenthesis. [a] significant at 1%, [b] significant at 5%, [c] significant at 10%

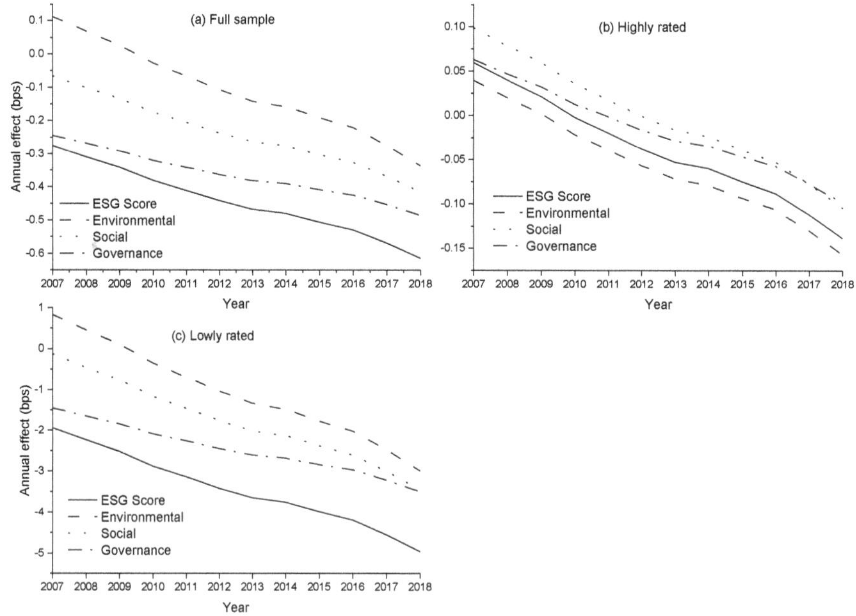

Fig. 1 Time-varying annual effects of each ESG score by rating grade. *Notes* Figures illustrate the time-varying annual effects of each ESG score on credit spreads induced by the development of ESG investments measured by the number of PRI signatories using the full sample (a), highly-rated issuer sample, i.e., above A-rated categories (b), and lowly-rated issuer sample, i.e., below BBB-rated categories (c). The annual effects of each ESG score are drawn as solid lines; while the dashed, dotted, and chain lines represent the environmental, social, and governance scores, respectively

ESG scores on the credit spreads. Furthermore, our results also demonstrate that the increasing rates of the negative impacts for the BBB-rated or below firm group are much larger than those for the A-rated or above firm group. Thus, investors tend to see more value on the information about higher ESG scores for lowerly rated firms, as the development of ESG investments.

4.2 Effectiveness of ESG Categories

Thus far, we have estimated our specification using ESG pillar scores. However, each pillar covers the broad ESG categories impacting corporations.[9] In this subsection, we further investigate the impacts of each ESG category that formulates the three ESG pillars to examine which ESG categories drive the lowering effect on credit spreads.

[9] In fact, the ESG category score is a weighted average of each category based on the category weights which vary per industry for the environmental and social categories and remain the same across industries for governance.

The underlying categories are as follows: resource use, emission, and innovation, for the environmental; workforce, human rights, community, and product responsibility, for the social; and management, shareholders, CSR strategy, for the governance.

We employ the approach in the last subsection to consider the time-varying ESG effect and estimate Eq. (2) using the ESG category score for an ESG score. Figure 2 presents the annual effects of the underlying ESG categories that formulate the three ESG pillars by issuer's credit quality. The annual effect is calculated as in the last subsection to vary with the number of PRI signatories. Panels (a)–(c) are for the highly-rated issuer, i.e., A-rated or above firm group, while those of (d)–(f) are for the lowly-rated issuer sample, i.e., BBB-rated or below firm group. The estimates of the coefficients on the interaction term between the ESG category score and the number of PRI signatories are mostly statistically significant, but even at a 10% significance level, a few are not; the human rights category for highly-rated issuers and CSR strategy category for lowly-rated issuers.

It is evident from Fig. 2 that the magnitude of the reduction of credit spread by an increase in ESG scores has become larger recently for all ESG categories. This is consistent with the pattern presented in the last subsection. Moreover, Panels (d)–(f) show a larger magnitude of the reduction in credit spreads than Panels (a)–(c). For instance, the estimated reduction in credit spreads by an increase in the emission category score in 2018 is -0.116 basis points for the highly-rated issuer, while it is -2.089 basis points for the lowly-rated issuer. Thus, the reduction in credit spreads depends on the issuer's credit quality for all ESG categories, where the larger reduction is observed for the BBB-rated or below firm group.

An important finding is that the results for highly-rated issuers show a similar pattern in Panels (a)–(c), where the annual lowering effect on the credit spread is more or less uniform across categories; however, for lowly-rated issuers, it varies substantially across categories within each ESG pillar, as can be seen in Panels (d)–(f). When we investigate each category's credit spread lowering effect, a similar pattern emerges. In Panel (d), i.e., the environment pillar, the resource use category's lowering effect on credit spreads exceeds that of innovation. Especially in the social pillar, the human rights category's credit spread lowering effect is noticeable, exceeding that of all other categories. Likewise, in the governance pillar, the management category shows a larger impact on credit spreads than the other two categories.

Overall, the analysis of the ESG category indicates the heterogeneous pattern of the negative effects of the ESG scores on credit spreads across the issuer's credit quality. For the A-rated or above firm group, the emission, workforce, and CSR strategy categories are the most influential in lowering the credit spreads in the E, S, and G pillars, respectively. On the other hand, for the BBB-rated or below firm group, the resource use, human right, and management categories are distinctly emerging in each ESG pillar, respectively.

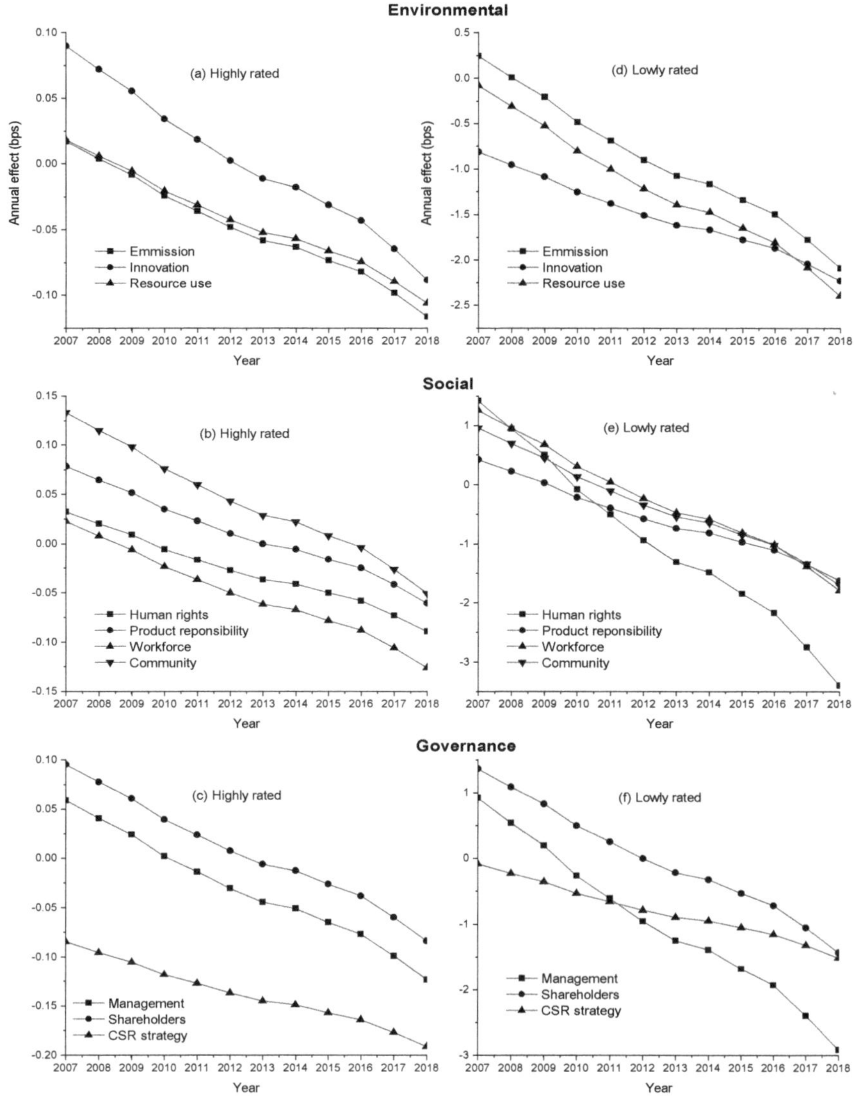

Fig. 2 Time-varying annual effects by rating grade and underlying ESG categories. *Notes* Figures show plots of the time-varying annual effects of the underlying ESG categories that formulate the three ESG pillars: environmental, social, and corporate governance. The sample of Panels (a)–(c) is the A-rated or above firm group, and that of Panels (d)–(f) is the BBB-rated or below firm group

5 Conclusions

This study presents evidence suggesting that ESG performance can be an important determinant of corporate bond credit spreads, an association that has not yet been well investigated in the literature. The sustainable finance product market is rapidly growing amid the coronavirus disease (COVID-19) pandemic, and new types of debt instruments have emerged: green, social, sustainability, and transition bonds. However, it is unclear how the market values corporate ESG performance and firms' credit risk.

An important feature of this study is the use of the firm-level credit spreads constructed from individual bond-level data by employing the bottom-up approach, which allows us to directly measure the link between corporate ESG performance and corporate bond credit spreads. The results in this study indicate that the higher corporate ESG performance significantly decreases corporate bond credit spreads, especially for lowly-rated firms. These results have potential implications for firms in connection to new issues of sustainable finance products in the bond market: lowly-rated firms can highlight their risk management and/or resilience to hedge ESG risks by attaining better ESG performance and may benefit from the lower fund-raising costs.

We also explore possible mechanisms through which company ESG performance affects corporate bond credit spreads. Results indicate heterogeneous impacts among ESG pillars as ESG investing develops in more recent years, particularly for the environmental issue, and it is more pronounced for lowly-rated firms. This finding is important for understanding the trend and characteristics of ESG investing. We acknowledge the role of the governance that is the core of corporate management; however, the market less evaluates governance issues, contrariwise, while the environmental issue arises from the recent global challenges against climate change. Regarding the time-varying impacts, the increasing rates of the negative impacts are considerably larger for lowly-rated firms than those for highly-rated firms. The results are also confirmed by the analysis using ESG category scores.

The findings of this study provide broad insights not only for asset pricing but also for macroeconomic policy. In September 2020, the European Central Bank stated that they would support sustainable finance and confront the climate change menace by accepting green bonds as collateral with payouts linked to sustainability targets and include them in its asset purchase schemes. This fast-growing green finance is irreversible, and COVID-19 is driving ESG investing in a social as well as a green agenda. This study documents the heterogeneous impacts of ESG performance on asset prices. Moreover, the impacts are shown to have become greater recently, and this trend is expected to grow. Therefore, our results relating to which of the ESG categories plays a key role in the market can be attributed to the different needs of the policymakers as well as market participants.

References

Acemoglu, D., Akcigit, U., Hanley, D., and Kerr, W. (2018). Transition to clean technology. *Journal of Political Economy*, 124(1):52–104.

Baker, M., Bergstresser, D., Serafeim, G., and Wurgler, J. (2018). Financing the response to climate change: The pricing and ownership of U.S. green bonds. NBER Working Paper 25194.

Boffo, R. and Patalano, R. (2020). ESG investing: Practices, progress and challenges. www.oecd.org/finance/ESG-Investing-Practices-Progress-and-Challenges.pdf OECD Paris.

Borgers, A., Derwall, J., Koedijk, K., and ter Horst, J. (2015). Do social factors influence investment behavior and performance? Evidence from mutual fund holdings. *Journal of Banking and Finance*, 60:112–126.

Bouslah, K., Kryzanowski, L., and M'Zali, B. (2013). The impact of the dimensions of social performance on firm risk. *Journal of Banking and Finance*, 37:1258–1273.

Colonnello, S., Curatola, G., and Gioffré, A. (2019). Pricing sin stocks: Ethical preference vs. risk aversion. *European Economic Review*, 118:69–100.

Derwall, J., Guenster, N., Bauer, R., and Koedijk, K. (2005). The ecoefficiency premium puzzle. *Financial Analysts Journal*, 61(2):51–63.

Dunbar, C., Li, Z. F., and Shi, Y. (2020). CEO risk-taking incentives and corporate social responsibility. *Journal of Corporate Finance*, 64:101714.

Dunbar, C., Li, Z. F., and Shi, Y. (2021). Corporate social (ir)responsibility and firm risk: The role of corporate governance. Available at SSRN: https://ssrn.com/abstract=3791594

Eccles, R. G., Ioannou, I., and Serafeim, G. (2014). The impact of corporate sustainability on organizational processes and performance. *Management Science*, 60:2835–2857.

Ederington, L., Yawitz, J., and Roberts, B. (1987). The information content of bond ratings. *Journal of Financial Research*, 10(3):211–237.

Fan, J. H. and Michalski, L. (2020). Sustainable factor investing: Where doing well meets doing good. *International Review of Economics and Finance,*, 70:230–256.

Faust, J., Gilchrist, S., Wright, J. H., and Zakrajšek, E. (2013). Credit spreads as predictors of real-time economic activity: A Bayesian model-averaging approach. *Review of Economics and Statistics*, 95(5):1501–1519.

Favara, G., Gilchrist, S., Lewis, K. F., and Zakrajšek, E. (2016). Recession risk and the excess bond premium. FEDS Notes. Washington: Board of Governors of the Federal Reserve System, April 8, 2016.

Gibson Brandon, R. and Krüger, P. (2018). The sustainability footprint of institutional investors. European Corporate Governance Institute - Finance Working Paper No. 571/2018.

Gilchrist, S., Yankov, V., and Zakrajšek, E. (2009). Credit market shocks and economic fluctuations: Evidence from corporate bond and stock markets. *Journal of Monetary Economics*, 56(4):471–493.

Gilchrist, S. and Zakrajšek, E. (2012). Credit spreads and business cycle fluctuations. *American Economic Review*, 102(4):1692–1720.

Haščič, I. and Migotto, M. (2015). Measuring environmental innovation using patent data. OECD Environment Working Papers No.89.

Hoepner, A. G. F., Oikonomou, I., Sautner, Z., Starks, L. T., and Zhou, X. (2020). ESG shareholder engagement and downside risk. European Corporate Governance Institute - Finance Working Paper No. 671/2020.

Hong, H. and Kacperczyk, M. (2009). The price of sin: The effects of social norms on markets. *Journal of Financial Economics*, 93(1):15–36.

Hong, H. and Kostovetsky, L. (2012). Red and blue investing: Values and finance. *Journal of Financial Economics*, 103(1):1–19.

Humphrey, J. E. and Lee, D. D. (2011). Australian socially responsible funds: Performance, risk and screening intensity. *Journal of Business Ethics*, 102(4):519–535.

Jang, G.-Y., Kang, H.-G., Lee, J.-Y., and Bae, K. (2020). ESG scores and the credit market. *Sustainability*, 12(8):1–13.

Jiraporn, P., Jiraporn, N., Boeprasert, A., and Chang, K. (2014). Does corporate social responsibility (CSR) improve credit ratings? Evidence from geographic identification. *Financial Management*, 43(3):505–531.

Kitzmueller, M. and Shimshack, J. (2012). Economic perspectives on corporate social responsibility. *Journal of Economic Literature*, 50(1):51–84.

Krueger, P., Sautner, Z., and Starks, L. T. (2020). The importance of climate risks for institutional investors. *Review of Financial Studies*, 33(3):1067–1111.

Lins, K. V., Servaes, H., and Tamayo, A. (2017). Social capital, trust, and firm performance: The value of corporate social responsibility during the financial crisis. *Journal of Finance*, 72(4):1785–1824.

Longstaff, F. A., Mithal, S., and Neis, E. (2005). Corporate yield spreads: Default risk or liquidity? New evidence from the credit default swap market. *Journal of Finance*, 60(5):2213–2253.

Managi, S., Okimoto, T., and Matsuda, A. (2012). Do socially responsible investment indexes outperform conventional indexes? *Applied Financial Economics*, 22(18):1511–1527.

Merton, R. C. (1974). On the pricing of corporate debt: The risk structure of interest rates. *Journal of Finance*, 29(2):449–470.

Nofsinger, J. and Varma, A. (2014). Socially responsible funds and market crises. *Journal of Banking and Finance*, 48:180–193.

OECD (2020). *OECD Business and Finance Outlook 2020: Sustainable and Resilient Finance*. OECD Publishing, Paris. https://doi.org/10.1787/eb61fd29-en

Pastor, L., Stambaugh, R. F., and Taylor, L. A. (2020). Sustainable investing in equilibrium. *Journal of Financial Economics*.

Rjiba, H., Jahmane, A., and Abid, I. (2020). Corporate social responsibility and firm value: Guiding through economic policy uncertainty. *Finance Research Letters*, 35:101553.

Stellner, C., Klein, C., and Zwergel, B. (2015). Corporate social responsibility and Eurozone corporate bonds: The moderating role of country sustainability. *Journal of Banking and Finance*, 59:538–549.

Stock, J. H. and Watson, M. W. (2003). Forecasting output and inflation: The role of asset prices. *Journal of Economic Literature*, 41(3):788–829.

Suto, M. and Takehara, H. (2020). Corporate social responsibility intensity, management earnings forecast accuracy, and investor trust: Evidence from japan. *Corporate Social Responsibility and Environmental Management*, 27(6):3047–3059.

Tirole, J. (2017). The governance and social responsibility of business. In *Economics for the Common Good*, chapter 7, pages 174–192. Princeton University Press, Princeton.

Wang, J., Chen, X., Li, X., Yu, J., and Zhong, R. (2020). The market reaction to green bond issuance: Evidence from China. *Pacific-Basin Finance Journal*, 60:101294.

Wu, L. and Zhang, F. X. (2008). A no-arbitrage analysis of macroeconomic determinants of the credit spread term structure. *Management Science*, 54(6):1160–1175.

Credit Default Swaps and Corporate Environmental Impacts in Japan

Tatsuyoshi Okimoto and Sumiko Takaoka

1 Introduction

In contrast to the time when Friedman (1970) stated that a corporate executive, who is an agent of the corporation owner, serves the interests of their principal, firms are now responsible for corporate greenhouse gas (GHG) emissions. The investor expects firms to disclose not only GHG emissions, but also the degree of climate-related risk that might impact their business financially. Climate-related risk includes transition and physical risks, which firms find difficult to measure and incorporate into their financial statements. Simultaneously, the market focuses on corporate performance in environmental challenges. For example, firms attempt to curb carbon emissions, and the market then tries to incorporate their performance into the evaluation of the firm.

Although the countries involved promised to reduce GHG emissions in the Paris Agreement, an international treaty on climate change that entered into force on November 4, 2016, their plans to avert a rise in global temperatures seem insufficient. Despite the top two emitter countries, China and the United States, joining the Paris Agreement, the global trend did not indicate a downward slope in GHG emissions (Fig. 1).

The market expects firms to not only reduce carbon emissions but also to disclose information about the climate risk that they might be exposed to in the entire process of their business operations. That is, decarbonization has become an urgent priority for corporate leaders in recent years, and requires switching to carbon-neutral or carbon-free energy sources. Moreover, investors must know the environmental

T. Okimoto (✉)
Faculty of Economics, Keio University and Research Institute of Economy, Trade and Industry (RIETI), Tokyo, Japan
e-mail: tatsuyoshi.okimoto@gmail.com

S. Takaoka
Faculty of Business Administration, Seikei University, Tokyo, Japan
e-mail: takaoka@bus.seikei.ac.jp

S. Takaoka (ed.), *Environmental Technology Innovation and ESG Investment*,
https://doi.org/10.1007/978-981-99-9768-8_3

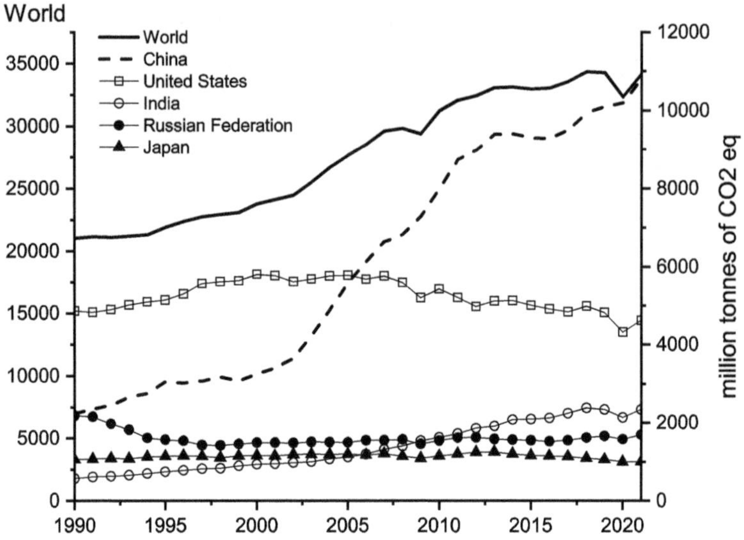

Fig. 1 Five largest GHG emitter countries. *Notes* This figure plots GHG emissions in million tonnes of CO_2 equivalent ($MtCO_2e$) of the world (left axis) and the five largest emitter countries (right axis): China, the United States, India, Russian Federation, and Japan. Observations span the years 1990–2021. *Data Source* International Energy Agency; graph drawn by one of the authors

impact of firms. Figure 2 displays carbon emissions by the Japanese sector group for the years 1990 and 2021. All sector groups reduced their carbon emissions; however, no drastic shifts were observed. Even if the expansion of economic production between 1990 and 2021 is considered, the pace of carbon emission reduction must be accelerated.

This chapter focuses on Japanese firms in the Asia-Pacific region and the effects of their environmental impact on credit default swap (CDS) spreads. This chapter focuses on Japan because it is the host country of the Third Session of the Conference of the Parties to the United Nations Framework Convention on Climate Change (COP3) held in Kyoto in December 1997, and Bill for the Promotion of Measures to Tackle Global Warming was submitted to the National Diet of Japan on April 28, 1998; thus, Japan and Japanese firms have a history of management against global warming long enough for time-series analysis. This study reveals how the market perceives the environmental impact of Japanese firms based on corporate CDS spreads, a widely recognized measure of the market perception of firms' default risk. If the market perceives that high environmental impact is critical for a firm's sustainable growth in their business, its credit risk is regarded as high. Conversely, when the market perceives that the environmentally friendly policy of the firm is costly and reduces the firm's profit, a high environmental impact can lower its credit risk.

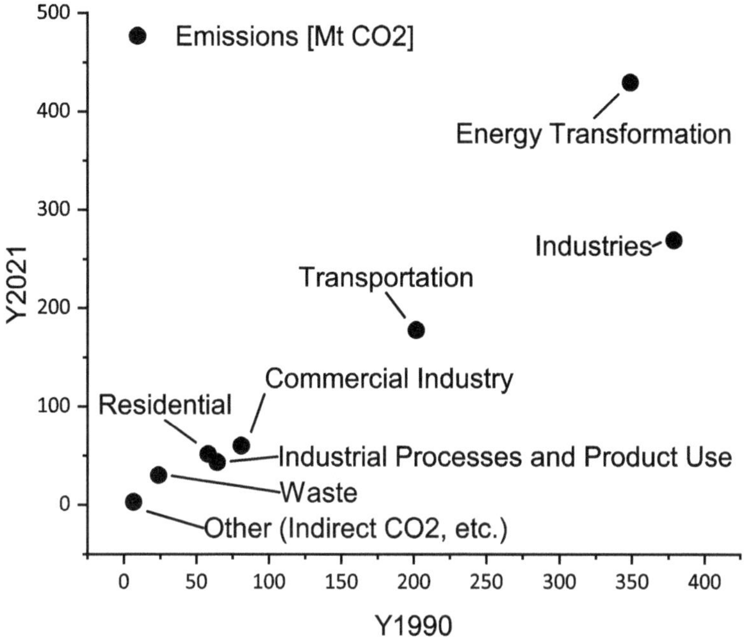

Fig. 2 CO_2 emissions in 1990 and in 2021 by Japanese sector groups. *Notes* This figure plots the CO_2 emissions (Mt CO_2) in the year 1990 against CO_2 emissions (Mt CO_2) in the year 2021 by Japanese sector categories; Energy Transformation, Industries, Transportation, Commercial Industry, Residential, Industrial Processes and Product Use, Waste, and Other (Indirect CO_2, etc.). *Data Source* Greenhouse Gas Inventory Office of Japan, National Institute for Environmental Studies; graph drawn by one of the authors

Recent research on mechanisms to promote clean inputs and technology has proposed policy intervention by means of carbon taxes and research subsidies. For example, Acemoglu et al. (2012) discussed government intervention through a system of carbon taxes and research subsidies to redirect firms' innovation toward clean inputs. Acemoglu et al. (2018) showed that the policy structure depending on both carbon taxes and research subsidies helps transition to clean technology. Aghion et al. (2016) emphasized the importance of carbon taxes to allow clean technologies to replace dirty technologies using the patent data of the car industry. As more investors expect that the carbon tax levy or regulation cost of large emitters will shrink their profit and value, they require a carbon risk premium or higher returns to invest in firms with high carbon emissions. Additionally, as consumers have become increasingly sensitive to the firm's challenge of reducing carbon emissions, with a preference for buying environmentally friendly products and/or services, the sustainable growth of high-carbon emitter firms is more unlikely. This implies that the CDS spread, which is the market perception of firms' sustainability, of larger carbon emitters is expected to be higher if carbon risk is recognized. Kölbel et al. (2022) show that disclosing transition risks increases CDS spreads after the Paris Climate Agreement of 2015 while disclosing physical risks decreases the spreads by using an AI-based algorithm.

The second goal is to investigate whether a firm's environmental impact is priced equally across maturities in the Japanese CDS market. As the global expansion of environmental, social, and governance (ESG) investing over the last decade has made the environmental strategy of a firm a pressing task in corporate management, climate risk can be considered a short-term risk rather than a long-term risk, or an important risk equally across maturities. While Drudi et al. (2021) stated that investor awareness of climate risk appears incomplete, studies such as Krueger et al. (2020) and Fahmy (2022) showed that institutional investors incorporate climate risk into their investments and perceive it as an important investment risk. Therefore, given the ESG investment growth, we assume that the environmental impact of the firm is critical, even for its long-term performance with respect to sustainable growth in the global market.

The main contribution of this study is that it examines the existence of an environmental impact premium in CDS markets and shows that the corporate environmental impact on CDS spreads is mostly significant for speculative-grade firms. Most market-based trading studies analyzed stock returns. For example, Bolton and Kacperczyk (2021a) supported the carbon risk premium hypothesis in stock returns in U.S. by confirming that stock returns are positively related to the level of carbon emissions; Oestreich and Tsiakas (2015) suggested the existence of carbon premium in German stock returns; Bolton and Kacperczyk (2021b) find carbon risk premium in all sectors of Asia, Europe, and North America; Ilhan et al. (2021) found that the carbon tail risk is priced in option; Hsu et al. (2019) showed a positive (negative) relationship between toxic emissions and stock returns (future profitability); In et al. (2010) indicated that investing in carbon-efficient firms can be profitable. Although Barth et al. (2022) indicated that higher ESG ratings mitigate the credit risks of US and European firms, few studies have examined the CDS markets. Therefore, we contribute to the literature by providing new empirical evidence on the environmental risk premiums in CDS markets.

Credit risk is a fundamental factor in corporate debt pricing; hence, this study also relates to another strand of the literature on the effect of climate or environmental risk on a firm's fund-raising costs, such as loans and bonds. For example, Chava (2014) suggested that lenders charge a significantly higher interest rate on bank loans issued to firms with environmental concerns, Delis et al. (2019) documented that fossil fuel reserves are priced in the loan market, Ehlers et al. (2022) found a carbon premium on syndicated loans, Kacperczyk and Peydro (2022) indicated that firms with higher carbon footprints borrowing from committed banks subsequently receive less bank credit. Regarding carbon risk in corporate bond issuances, for example, Flammer (2021) showed that green bond investors respond positively to issuance announcements of green bonds, and Cao et al. (2021) found that bonds issued by high-carbon firms experience worse liquidity conditions. Our findings provide evidence that environmental risk is priced in credit default spreads and affects corporate debt pricing.

Another contribution of this study is its investigation of issuers' different environmental impacts on credit risk. The growing pressure from investors regarding ESG-related risk through their investments is notably prominent, and several studies suggest that ESG investing has a considerable impact on asset prices. For example, Hong and Kacperczyk (2009) found that "sin" stocks (alcohol, tobacco, and gaming), which are disinvestment targets of ESG investing, receive less coverage from analysts and have higher returns than otherwise comparable stocks. Gibson et al. (2018) measured the portfolio-level environmental and social characteristics of institutional investors and show that the environmental and social portfolio policies can reduce the portfolio risk. The theoretical model in Colonnello et al. (2019) suggests an ethical preference-based model to study stock anomalies and discloses nonpecuniary factors in the formation of investment decisions and asset prices. The literature on ESG and bond markets has also been expanding recently, for example, Stellner et al. (2015) on Eurozone corporate bonds, Jang et al. (2020) on ESG scores and bond returns in Korea, Huynh and Xia (2021) on climate change news risk and corporate bond returns in the US, and Okimoto and Takaoka (2024) on Japanese corporate bond spreads. Furthermore, the survey results of Stroebel and Wurgler (2021) show that respondents believe that asset prices underestimate climate risks rather than overestimate them, whereas Duan et al. (2022) indicated that carbon-emission risk is underpriced in the corporate bond market, a phenomenon referred to as investor underreaction. Despite these findings, the credit quality of listed firms in the market differs substantially. We have two different views on the relationship between credit quality and the environmental impact on CDS spreads. One view is that the market has overlooked the growth of ESG investments of firms over the last decade or so; thus, the improvement of environmental risk is not priced on CDS spreads for high credit quality firms whose credit spreads for corporate bonds were low; thus, they do not reflect the improvement or change in corporate environmental impact. Another view is that regulated institutional investors target highly rated investment-grade firms. Thus, CDS spreads for firms outside the targets of such investors naturally underreact to pressure for environmental risk. We empirically investigate these two views by focusing on credit rating categories and sector characteristics. Specifically, this study contributes to the literature by investigating the different environmental impacts of credit quality on CDS spreads. This is an interesting contribution because most previous studies implicitly assumed a constant environmental risk impact on asset prices across credit quality.

The main findings of this study can be summarized as follows. We begin our analysis by exploring the pricing of the environmental impact ratio, which is monetarized environmental quantities divided by revenue, on CDS spreads using data on Japanese firms. These firms have long and actively engaged in efficient energy utilization to mitigate global warming concerns and fulfill the Japanese government's commitment under the Kyoto Protocol to reduce GHG emissions.[1] Our first finding is that none of the direct impact ratios, indirect impact ratios, or direct and indirect impact ratios are priced in the CDS spreads when we do not control for the credit quality of the firm. This is not surprising, because the credit spreads for highly rated firms or even investment-grade firms are lowered by the central bank's monetary easing measures.

Second, the environmental impact ratio is priced in CDS spreads for speculative-grade firms. For these firms, the direct, indirect, and direct and indirect impact ratios have increasing effects on CDS spreads; that is, a higher environmental impact ratio increases CDS spreads. The effect is significant even after controlling for credit ratings, illiquidity, financial conditions of the firm, and sector*year fixed effects. This result supports the view that CDS spreads for speculative-grade firms are more sensitive to environmental risk than those for investment-grade firms.

Next, we examine the sectoral effect of the environmental impact ratio on CDS spreads. Sectors in which firms operate are classified as hard-to-abate or non-hard-to-abate. Our third finding is that the CDS spreads for firms operating in hard-to-abate sector increase only with an increase in the direct environmental impact ratio. This reflects that attention to the hard-to-abate sector focuses mostly on their direct environmental impact, because the reduction in carbon emissions or environmental impact by hard-to-abate sectors contributes to the reduction in the indirect environmental impact of the firms in their supply chain. Additionally, firms in hard-to-abate sectors depend on industrial processes that employ extremely high temperatures for production or high-density energy sources; hence, the high environmental impact ratio in such sectors is regarded as not ready for net-zero emissions. Firms in such sectors can gain recognition and lower their CDS spreads by reducing their environmental impact.

Finally, we show that the environmental impact ratio affects the CDS spread curve for speculative-grade firms: short- and long-term spreads. Each environmental impact ratio (direct impact, indirect impact, or direct and indirect impact ratio) is associated with the CDS spread curve and short- and long-term CDS spreads. These results represent the investors' perception that high environmental impact is regarded as a factor of credit risk across maturities, which implies that investors are suspicious of the long-term sustainable growth of a firm with high environmental impact; in turn, speculative-grade firms can lower their CDS spreads by decreasing the environmental impact ratio for both short- and long-term fundraising.

The remainder of this chapter is organized as follows. Section 2 introduces the datasets used in the empirical analysis. Section 3 explains our hypotheses and the empirical strategy for the analysis of CDS spreads, and discusses the results. Section 4

[1] For example, Japan ranks first in the share of the world's high-value inventions (international patent families with size two or greater) in environment-related technologies from 2009 to 2011 according to Haščič and Migotto (2015).

explores the effects of carbon emissions on the CDS spread curve. Section 5 presents concluding remarks. The appendix contains the definitions of the variables and illiquidity measure construction.

2 Data and Sample Construction

The dataset used in this analysis consists mainly of CDS spread, firms' environmental impact, and corporate financial data. Our dataset covers a time range from 2005 to 2019, imposed by the availability of firm-level environmental impact data.

Our dependent variable is firms' CDS spreads, which are the market prices of the underlying firms' default probabilities. As CDS contracts are made over the counter, their maturity is negotiable, ranging from a few months to 10 years or longer.[2] To construct the firm-level CDS spread index, we obtain year-end CDS spreads from Markit, where the original dataset contains daily spreads. We follow the approach proposed by Gilchrist et al. (2009) and Gilchrist and Zakrajšek (2012) to construct a spread index at the firm level, and calculate the arithmetic average of a firm's year-end CDS spreads for its outstanding contracts. Specifically, an individual firm's CDS spread for contracts with different maturities from the same firm is given as

$$CDS_{it} = \frac{1}{N_{it}} \sum_{k} s_{it}[k], \tag{1}$$

where $s_{it}[k]$ is the CDS spread for contract k for the underlying firm i in year t and N_{it} is the number of contracts with different maturities.

For the company's environmental impact ratio data, we obtained three firm-level environmental impact ratio data from Trucost's Environmental Register database, which is one of the largest carbon emission and related databases. Trucost's data began in 2005 and cover listed equity companies but not all companies in Japan. The data used in this analysis for the corporate environmental impact ratio are the Total-Direct Impact Ratio (%), Total-Indirect Impact Ratio (%), and Total-Direct + Indirect Impact Ratio (%). Appendix A contains details of each variable used in the estimation. The Total-Direct Impact Ratio (%) is the total direct external cost divided by revenue, where the direct external environmental impacts are the impact of a company on the environment through its own activities. The Total-Indirect Impact Ratio (%) refers to the total indirect external cost divided by revenue, which covers environmental impact through the goods and services that firms purchase, known as supply chain or indirect impacts. The Total-Direct + Indirect Impact Ratio (%) refers to the total direct and indirect external cost divided by revenue, which is the sum of all direct and indirect external environmental costs of the company, and is expressed as a percentage of revenue. The Total-Direct + Indirect impact ratio is the largest proportion of a company's environmental impact ratio.

[2] Refer to Longstaff et al. (2005) for a detailed explanation of credit default swaps.

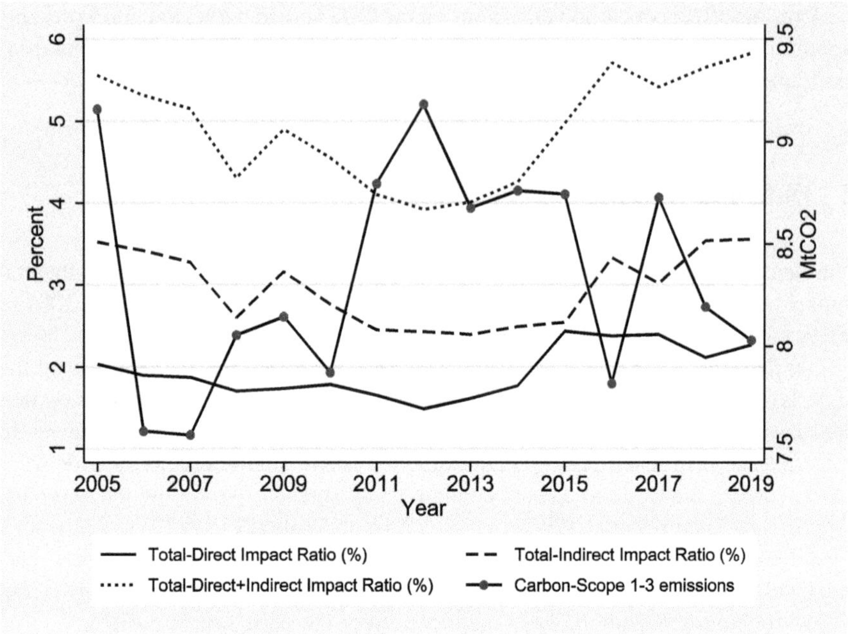

Fig. 3 Time-series plot of Environmental impact ratio and carbon emissions. *Notes* This figure displays the yearly average of Total-Direct Impact Ratio (%), Total-Indirect Impact Ratio (%), Total-Direct + Indirect Impact Ratio (%), and corporate Scope 1, Scope 2, and Scope 3 emissions in our CDS sample over the period 2005–2019

Each environmental impact ratio data point is equally important; hence, we use all three variables in the analysis. However, each variable is used alternatively in the estimation because of collinearity. Figure 3 plots the three average corporate environmental impact ratios with corporate Scope 1, Scope 2, and Scope 3 emissions over the sample period from 2005 to 2019. While the average corporate emissions fluctuate, each environmental impact ratio shows a slight upward trend. The plot indicates that the Total-Indirect Impact Ratio (%) is consistently higher than the Total-Direct Impact Ratio (%). The magnitude of each environmental impact ratio depends on the sector characteristics and changes over time; hence, we controlled for the sector-year effects in the estimation.

We match firm-level CDS spread data and corporate environmental impact ratio data with the firm's financial dataset, which includes credit rating and financial indicators, to control for financial health and credit quality. Following previous studies, such as Stellner et al. (2015), the financial indicators include the firm's earnings before interest and taxes (EBIT) margin (EBIT/total revenue), debt/capital, capital expenditure (CapEx)/total revenue, return on invested capital (ROIC), equity price volatility, and Earnings Per Share (EPS). Furthermore, the issuer's credit rating information is used to control credit quality. The firm's information is taken from the Thomson

Reuters database immediately prior to the year-end CDS spread. Table 1 presents the Definitions of Variables for the panel dataset used in this analysis. The universe of Trucost's data for Japanese firm observations expanded in 2016, whereas that of the CDS dataset did not. This enables our sample mean for data drawn from Trucost's Environmental Register database to remain unaffected by the sudden expansion of the Trucost sample; for example, the sudden drop in average carbon emissions before and after the expansion of the universe in Trucost's data for Japanese firms.

3 Corporate Environmental Impact Ratio and CDS Spread

In this section, we empirically explore the relationship between corporate environmental impact ratios and CDS spreads.

3.1 Hypotheses

This subsection presents the hypotheses to be empirically examined. There are several underlying mechanisms by which the environmental impact ratio affects the CDS spread. Given that the clientele of the CDS market are mostly institutional investors who are well informed about firms and the market, we consider the following hypotheses. Importantly, these hypotheses are neither mutually exclusive nor conflicting.

H1: Environmental risk hypothesis

As the climate-related risks are prominent in corporate management, the regulation and tax system on fossil fuels are to be further tightened on a global basis. Firms with a high environmental impact ratio are exposed to climate-related risks including carbon risk. The tighter regulations and higher carbon tax may decrease the net profit of such firms, which leads to their lower asset prices. Investors evaluate such firms less regarding their sustainability, resulting in higher CDS spreads.

CDS market participants are mostly well-informed institutional investors, meaning they are forward looking and sensitive to event-specific risks. Climate-related risks are becoming increasingly relevant to firms' future operations. As investors expect the carbon tax levy or regulation cost for firms with a high environmental impact ratio to shrink their profits and value, the CDS spread for such firms is expected to be higher because of such high environmental risk.

Additionally, investors' ESG preferences in Pastor et al. (2021) and taste premiums in Zerbib (2019, 2022) as well as global trends in investor awareness, for example, Drudi et al. (2021) and Fahmy (2022) appear to be irreversible. The rise in investors' awareness of climate risk, especially after the Paris Agreement, has made them more concerned about climate-related risks.

Table 1 Descriptive statistics

		Mean	Std. dev.	Min	Max	N/n/$\bar{T}$
CDS spread (bp)	Overall	81.60	154.47	3.59	3629.58	3215.00
	Between		111.44	11.66	1254.12	293.00
	Within		122.85	−1133.27	2457.05	10.97
Total-direct impact ratio (%)	Overall	2.02	6.02	0.00	112.67	3215.00
	Between		4.72	0.00	37.05	293.00
	Within		3.42	−28.55	96.55	10.97
Total-indirect impact ratio (%)	Overall	2.99	4.88	0.21	85.96	3215.00
	Between		6.75	0.23	70.42	293.00
	Bithin		1.10	−26.31	18.54	10.97
Total-direct + indirect impact ratio (%)	Overall	5.01	8.03	0.22	115.83	3215.00
	Between		8.46	0.24	70.94	293.00
	Within		3.63	−25.78	98.98	10.97
EPS	Overall	180.29	915.88	0.00	25185.00	3215.00
	Between		1223.49	0.78	19920.92	293.00
	Within		205.81	−4524.63	5444.37	10.97
EBIT to revenue	Overall	0.08	0.10	−1.27	0.69	3215.00
	Between		0.08	−0.14	0.60	293.00
	Within		0.07	−1.06	0.59	10.97
Debt to capital	Overall	0.57	0.46	0.00	11.97	3215.00
	Between		0.41	0.00	3.64	293.00
	Within		0.26	−1.07	10.52	10.97
Capex to revenue	Overall	0.07	0.09	0.00	1.81	3215.00
	Between		0.08	0.00	1.02	293.00
	Within		0.05	−0.56	1.35	10.97
Price volatility	Overall	26.22	6.96	6.88	57.90	3215.00
	Between		6.45	7.03	46.60	293.00
	Within		3.37	11.61	43.48	10.97
ROIC	Overall	4.13	5.33	−62.73	63.34	3215.00
	Between		3.14	−6.90	16.95	293.00
	Within		4.61	−62.67	63.40	10.97
Credit rating						
AAA rating	1%					
AA rating	15%					
A rating	42%					
BBB rating	24%					
BB rating	11%					
B rating	4%					
CCC rating	3%					

Notes The table presents the summary statistics for the unbalanced panel data from 2005 to 2019. N, n, and $\bar{T}$ refer to the observations with firm-year data, the number of firms, and the average number of years per firm, respectively. Credit rating indicates the ratio of credit rating categories assigned to the firm in our estimation sample

This hypothesis is also related to theories that ESG-conscious investors prefer green firms' stocks, or sustainable investors prefer green firms to brown firms. Heinkel et al. (2001) theoretically indicated that the polluting firms' cost of capital can be raised by green investors. The theoretical model of Luo and Balvers (2017) considers the boycott risk premium of socially responsible investors. If firms with a high environmental impact ratio are targeted, their asset prices must pay extra compensation for the risk. Pastor et al. (2021) developed the theoretical model that considers ESG criteria and indicates that greener firms have higher market values, thereby lowering the cost of capital for green firms. Pedersen et al. (2021) also showed that prices of green stocks are relatively higher than brown stocks' prices.

H2: Underreaction hypothesis

The market overlooked the growth of ESG investments of the firm over the last decade or so, thus the improvement of environmental risk is not priced on CDS spreads for the firms.

One motivation for this hypothesis is the market underreaction discussed in Pedersen et al. (2021) and Duan et al. (2022). Specifically, Pedersen et al. (2021) argued that although ESG performance could be a favorable signal of firm fundamentals, the market could underreact to this predictability of corporate ESG performance for expected future profits because of the lack of recognition. Duan et al. (2022) also argued that fewer investors underreact when investor awareness increases.

Even though the disaster and climate crisis risks stemming from climate change are extensively recognized worldwide, the market has overlooked the growth of ESG investments of the firm over the last decade. In particular, a lengthy period of monetary easing in developed countries (the US, UK, Euro Area, and Japan) lowered the credit spreads for corporate bonds issued by high-rated or investment-grade firms because of unconventional monetary policy measures, which do not reflect the improvement or change in corporate environmental impact by further lowering the credit spreads.

Moreover, given the long history of the Energy-Saving Act in Japan, the media has repeatedly reported that Japanese firms have a thoroughgoing energy conservation policy and create environmental technologies. Given the relatively high decarbonization cost in Japan, as indicated in OECD (2019), investors might be concerned about profitability as a firm accelerates its decarbonization.

3.2 Baseline Results

First, we investigate the connection between corporate environmental impact ratios and CDS spreads by assuming that the impacts are constant across a firm's credit quality as a baseline. Figure 4 plots carbon emissions from the five largest emitter sectors from 1990 to 2021. This graph indicates that the five largest emitter sectors were the same in these three decades and that the order of the largest emitter sectors was also the same. This indicates that we must control for sector characteristics in the estimation.

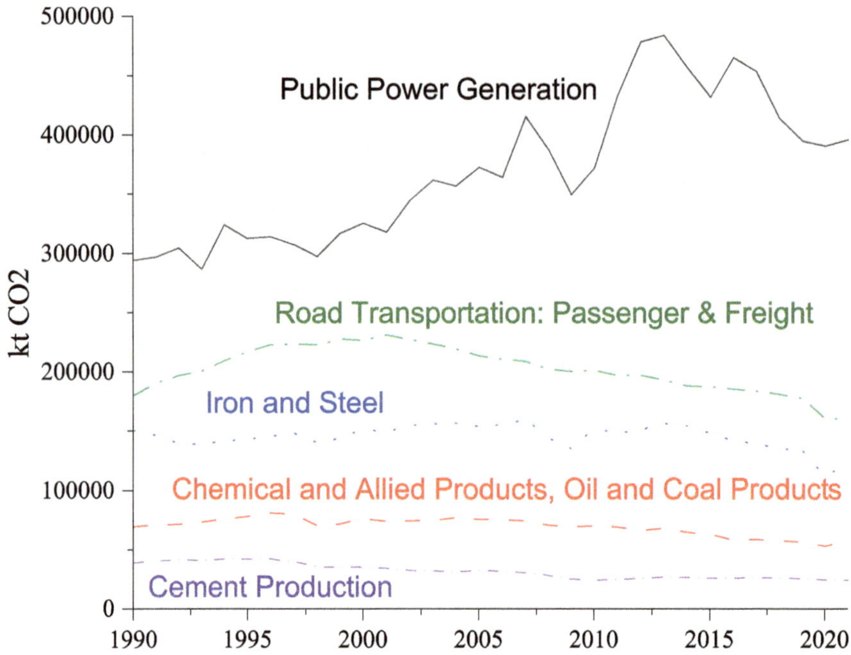

Fig. 4 Five largest sectors of CO_2 emissions in Japan. *Notes* This figure plots the CO_2 emissions (kt: kilotons) of the five largest emitter sectors in Japan. Observations span the years 1990–2021. *Data Source* Greenhouse Gas Inventory Office of Japan, National Institute for Environmental Studies; graph drawn by one of the authors

In the specification of the estimation models, we include firm fixed effects and sector*year fixed effects, thereby controlling for unobserved firm-level and absorbing all time-varying, observed, and unobserved sector heterogeneity. We estimate the following specifications.

$$\text{CDS}_{it} = \alpha_i + \alpha_{ts} + \beta_0 \text{Environmental Impact ratio}_{it} + \lambda \text{Controls}_{it} + \epsilon_{it}, \quad (2)$$

where the dependent variable is the CDS spread of firm i in year t (asinh(CDS spread on the basis point)), and the environmental impact ratio of firm i in year t is used as the main variable of interest. The model specification contains firm fixed effects α_i and sector*year fixed effects α_{ts}. The inverse hyperbolic sine transformation of CDS spreads is used to control for heteroskedasticity as a similar transformation, commonly taking the logarithm of corporate bond credit spreads when the distribution of credit spreads is highly skewed. Additionally, all the level variables were transformed using an inverse hyperbolic sine.

We denote the coefficient of interest as β_0. We consider the environmental risk hypothesis (**H1**) to be supported if β_0 is significantly positive. By contrast, for the underreaction hypothesis (**H2**), we expect that the environmental impact ratio has no significant impact on CDS spreads; that is, β_0 is not statistically significant if the underreaction hypothesis holds.

To control for the factors determining the CDS spreads, $Controls_{it}$ contains the firm's credit rating information, a vector of financial variables containing useful information on the default probability of the firm. Illiquidity is also a pricing factor in the CDS market, which is documented in e.g. Guo and Newton (2013) and Gehde-Trapp et al. (2018). We calculate and include the illiquidity measure in our estimation specifications. Appendix B presents the calculation of the illiquidity measure.

Our empirical strategy for determining the relationship between the corporate environmental impact ratio and CDS spreads begins with the panel estimation of Eq. (2). One might be concerned about the causality of the association between the corporate environmental impact ratio and CDS spreads; however, CDS spreads are event-specific and inherently forward looking. Thus, reverse causality between CDS spreads and the corporate environmental impact ratio seems unlikely, and we can reasonably overlook this issue. Additionally, we use year-end CDS spreads to minimize simultaneity issues, predetermining many of the explanatory variables.

Table 2 reports the estimation results of Eq. (2) using the firm-level environmental impact ratio for (1) the Total-Direct Impact Ratio (%), (2) Total-Indirect Impact Ratio (%), and (3) Total-Direct + Indirect Impact Ratio (%), credit rating dummies, illiquidity measure, and financial indicators. As can be seen, none of the coefficients of the environmental impact ratio are significant, even at the 10% significance level. The results indicate that the underreaction hypothesis (**H2**) is supported, indicating that investors do not incorporate corporate environmental risk into the pricing of CDS spreads and that environmental risk does not affect corporate credit risk. One possible reason for this is that the environmental impact ratio has two effects on firms' credit risks. A higher corporate environmental impact increases firms' credit risk due to environmental risk, possibly because of more severe regulation of carbon emissions. However, a higher corporate environmental impact could signal lower default risk, reflecting higher economic activity. The results in Table 2 suggest that these two effects could offset investors' underreaction, supporting the underreaction hypothesis (**H2**). We examine this possibility more rigorously by controlling for credit quality and sectors in the following subsections.

Other control variables tend to have expected effects on CDS spreads. For example, the CDS spreads of AAA-rated firms are significantly lower. Similarly, better financial conditions (i.e., a lower debt-to-capital ratio) lead to significantly lower CDS spreads. EPS shows a significantly negative relationship with CDS spreads, suggesting that profitability generally lowers CDS spreads. In contrast, our results indicate that CDS spreads are significantly higher with various types of risks captured by illiquidity and price volatility. Although this study does not focus on the role of liquidity in the Japanese CDS market, the results provide evidence that illiquidity plays a role in pricing CDS spreads.

Table 2 CDS spread and environmental impacts of the firm

	Spread		
	(1) Direct	(2) Indirect	(3) Direct + Indirect
Impact ratio	−0.002	0.011	−0.001
	(0.002)	(0.008)	(0.002)
AAA rating	−0.055[a]	−0.054[a]	−0.055[a]
	(0.017)	(0.017)	(0.017)
AA rating	−0.037	−0.037	−0.037
	(0.025)	(0.025)	(0.025)
A rating	−0.013	−0.011	−0.013
	(0.052)	(0.052)	(0.052)
Illiquidity	0.033[a]	0.033[a]	0.033[a]
	(0.007)	(0.007)	(0.007)
EPS	−0.038[a]	−0.038[a]	−0.038[a]
	(0.011)	(0.011)	(0.011)
EBIT margin	0.049	0.051	0.050
	(0.144)	(0.144)	(0.144)
Debt/capital	0.185[b]	0.184[b]	0.184[b]
	(0.075)	(0.075)	(0.075)
Capex/revenue	−0.375[b]	−0.375[b]	−0.375[b]
	(0.186)	(0.186)	(0.186)
ROIC	−0.013	−0.013	−0.013
	(0.017)	(0.017)	(0.017)
Price volatility	0.017[a]	0.017[a]	0.017[a]
	(0.003)	(0.003)	(0.003)
Year*sector fixed effects	Yes	Yes	Yes
Firm fixed effects	Yes	Yes	Yes
Observations	3215	3215	3215
R^2	0.87	0.87	0.87

Notes The table presents the estimation results of Eq. (2) based on environmental impacts of the firm for (1) Total-Direct Impact Ratio (%), (2) Total-Indirect Impact Ratio (%), and (3) Total-Direct + Indirect Impact Ratio (%), illiquidity measure, rating dummies, and financial indicators. The baseline rating category is below BBB. All level variables are transformed using the inverse hyperbolic sine. Firm fixed effects and year*sector fixed effects are included. Standard errors (SE) clustered at the firm level are in parenthesis. [a] significant at 1%, [b] significant at 5%, [c] significant at 10%

3.3 Credit Quality

Thus far, we assumed a constant corporate environmental impact on CDS spreads across firms' credit quality. However, the movement of the CDS spreads differs substantially over time, as shown in Fig. 5. The difference in the CDS spreads between investment- and speculative-grade firms does not remain constant over time. Figure 5 shows the steep surge in CDS spreads for speculative-grade firms before the financial crises: the Lehman collapse and the European debt crisis. However, the CDS spreads for investment-grade firms do not display a large variation compared to speculative-grade firms. In contrast to the global financial crisis period of 2007–2011, the CDS spreads for speculative-grade firms are close to those for investment-grade firms after 2016. These fluctuations in CDS spreads indicate that the CDS spreads for the speculative-grade firms are more sensitive to risks than for the investment-grade firms.

In this subsection, we relax the assumption that the impact of the corporate environmental impact ratio on CDS spreads is constant across the credit quality of a firm, and then examine the impact on CDS spreads by credit quality on CDS spreads. Table 3 reports the mean and standard deviation of the CDS spread (bp), Total-Direct Impact Ratio (%), Total-Indirect Impact Ratio (%), and Total-Direct + Indirect Impact

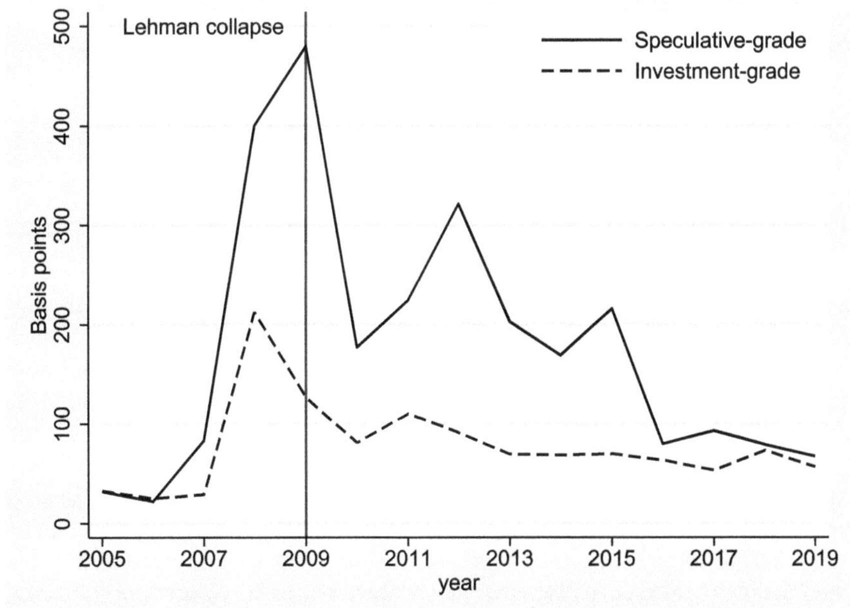

Fig. 5 Time-series plot of CDS spreads by credit quality. *Notes* This figure plots the time-series CDS spreads for investment-grade firms in dotted line and speculative-grade firms in solid line, respectively

Table 3 CDS spreads and environmental impact ratios by credit rating category

	Spread (bp)	Total-direct impact ratio (%)	Total-indirect impact ratio (%)	Total-direct + indirect impact ratio (%)
AAA rating				
Mean	50.79	2.18	2.68	4.86
Std. dev.	38.38	3.97	2.11	5.03
AA rating				
Mean	54.94	2.57	2.43	5.00
Std. dev.	73.97	7.12	3.16	8.22
A rating				
Mean	73.36	1.78	3.35	5.13
Std. dev.	138.21	4.47	5.63	7.46
BBB rating				
Mean	84.22	1.93	2.98	4.91
Std. dev.	110.51	6.25	5.47	8.58
BB rating				
Mean	98.45	2.41	2.72	5.13
Std. dev.	172.51	9.08	2.93	9.74
B rating				
Mean	206.67	1.80	2.42	4.22
Std. dev.	474.23	3.72	2.30	4.70
CCC rating				
Mean	136.33	1.78	2.68	4.46
Std. dev.	98.86	4.03	3.71	5.98

Notes The table reports the mean and standard deviation of CDS spreads (bp), Total-Direct Impact Ratio (%), Total-Indirect Impact Ratio (%), and Total-Direct + Indirect Impact Ratio (%) by credit rating category

Ratio (%) by credit rating category. The mean of the CDS spreads increases as credit quality decreases, except CCC ratings. The mean CDS spread for B-rated firms is higher than that for CCC-rated firms, but the standard deviation for B-rated firms is much larger than that for CCC-rated firms. Regarding the corporate environmental impact ratio and credit rating category, with an improvement in credit quality, there is no decreasing nor increasing tendency of the mean for each impact ratio: (1) Total-Direct Impact, (2) Total-Indirect Impact, and (3) Total-Direct + Indirect Impact. For example, the means of the Total-Direct + Indirect Impact Ratio (%) for the A- and BB-rating categories are the same. Thus, there is no relationship between credit quality and the corporate environmental impact ratio. We add the interaction of the environmental impact ratio and a speculative-grade dummy to Eq. (2) to differentiate the impact of the corporate environmental impact ratio on investment- and speculative-grade firms:

$$\begin{aligned}\text{CDS}_{it} = \alpha_i + \alpha_{ts} + \beta_0 &\text{Environmental Impact ratio}_{it} \\ &+ \beta_1 \text{Environmental Impact ratio}_{it} \times I(\text{Speculative-grade}_{it}) \\ &+ \lambda \text{Controls}_{it} + \epsilon_{it},\end{aligned} \quad (3)$$

where $I(Speculative\text{-}grade_{it})$ equals 1 if in year t the credit rating for firm i falls into the speculative grade.

Table 4 reports the estimation results, including the interaction term between credit quality and corporate environmental impact ratio. The results indicate that the coefficient of the corporate environmental impact ratio for investment-grade firms is significantly negative for (1) Total-Direct Impact. This negative coefficient can be explained by two factors. First, a higher corporate environmental impact could signal higher economic activity, thus significantly reducing the CDS spreads for (1) Total-Direct Impact. Second, investors require a lower risk premium for investment-grade companies because their default risk is considered small and they are less sensitive to environmental risk. For the same reasons, the coefficient of the corporate environmental impact ratio for investment-grade firms is insignificant for (2) Total-Indirect Impact, and (3) Total-Direct + Indirect Impact. We believe that the Indirect Impact is less directly related to firms' economic activity; thus, its reducing CDS spread impact is somewhat limited, making the coefficient insignificant. On the contrary, the interaction term between the corporate environmental impact ratio and speculative-grade dummy, β_1, is significantly positive, regardless of the environmental impact. This implies that, compared to investment-grade firms, speculative-grade firms are required to pay significantly higher environmental risk premiums because they are more vulnerable to environmental risk due to higher default risk. Therefore, we find evidence for the environmental risk hypothesis (**H1**) only for speculative-grade firms.

In summary, our results suggest that environmental risk causes substantial damage to speculative-grade firms when it materializes. Speculative-grade firms' financial health is vulnerable to risk, whereas the financial condition of investment-grade firms are more resilient to risk. Thus, the market perceives the magnitude of the environmental risk to be larger for speculative-grade firms. In other words, speculative-grade firms can lower their CDS spreads by reducing their environmental impact ratios more than investment-grade firms can.

3.4 Sectoral Impacts on CDS Spreads

We report evidence that the underreaction hypothesis (**H2**) is supported when we assume that the environmental impact ratio's impact on CDS spreads is constant across firms' credit quality. When we control for credit quality, the environmental risk hypothesis (**H1**) is supported for speculative-grade firms. In this subsection, we consider sectoral differences in addition to firms' credit quality.

When firms want to mitigate their environmental impact, the market and regulators regard hard-to-abate sectors as key, and focus their attention on firms in such

Table 4 CDS spreads and environmental impacts of the firm by credit quality

	Spread		
	(1) Direct	(2) Indirect	(3) Direct + Indirect
Impact ratio	−0.004[c] (0.002)	0.010 (0.008)	−0.003 (0.002)
Speculative-grade × Impact ratio	0.006[a] (0.002)	0.011[a] (0.004)	0.005[a] (0.002)
AAA rating	−0.051[a] (0.018)	−0.041[b] (0.019)	−0.045[b] (0.018)
AA rating	−0.031 (0.025)	−0.026 (0.026)	−0.026 (0.025)
A rating	−0.007 (0.052)	−0.001 (0.052)	−0.004 (0.052)
Illiquidity	0.033[a] (0.007)	0.033[a] (0.007)	0.033[a] (0.007)
EPS	−0.038[a] (0.011)	−0.037[a] (0.011)	−0.038[a] (0.011)
EBIT margin	0.049 (0.144)	0.049 (0.144)	0.048 (0.144)
Debt/capital	0.186[b] (0.075)	0.184[b] (0.074)	0.186[b] (0.075)
Capex/revenue	−0.377[b] (0.186)	−0.374[b] (0.186)	−0.376[b] (0.186)
ROIC	−0.012 (0.017)	−0.013 (0.017)	−0.013 (0.017)
Price volatility	0.017[a] (0.003)	0.017[a] (0.003)	0.017[a] (0.003)
Year*sector fixed effects	Yes	Yes	Yes
Firm fixed effects	Yes	Yes	Yes
Observations	3215	3215	3215
R^2	0.87	0.87	0.87

Notes The table presents the estimation results of Eq. (3). The credit quality is referred to as investment-grade when the firm's credit rating is above BBB, while the credit quality is referred to as speculative-grade when the firm's credit rating is below BB. Firm fixed effects and year*sector fixed effects are included. Standard errors (SE) clustered at the firm level are in parenthesis. [a] significant at 1%, [b] significant at 5%, [c] significant at 10%

sectors. Within or among sectors, there are firms whose operations fall in a sector with relatively higher abatement costs than in other sectors. The Energy Transitions Commission (2018) referred to heavy industry sectors and heavy duty transport as harder-to-abate sectors, and Teske et al. (2020) pointed out energy and utility sectors as key (supplier) sectors. In this section, we explicitly control for the effects of firms in such hard-to-abate sectors by classifying the firms into "non-hard-to-abate" sectors or "hard-to-abate" sectors. Following the literature, we classify the heavy industry (cement, steel, chemicals, and aluminum), heavy-duty transport (shipping, trucking, and aviation), energy, and utilities as hard-to-abate sectors, for example, The Energy Transitions Commission (2018). Decarbonizing hard-to-abate sectors can have the knock-on effect of driving down the indirect environmental impact of other firms throughout the supply chain, such as a reduction in Scope 3 emissions.

Although firms in hard-to-abate sectors find it difficult to decarbonize themselves because of the high costs of decarbonizing their businesses, energy sources, and integrated industrial processes, the sector's readiness to challenge climate risk is required in the market. Table 5 shows the mean and standard deviation of the CDS spreads and each impact ratio: (1) Total-Direct Impact, (2) Total-Indirect Impact, and (3) Total-Direct + Indirect Impact for firms in the non-hard-to-abate and hard-to-abate sectors. The CDS spreads for firms in hard-to-abate sectors are lower than those for firms in non-hard-to-abate sectors on average and with smaller standard deviations. In contrast, hard-to-abate sectors have a mean of Total-Direct Impact Ratio (%) that is much larger than that of non-hard-to-abate sectors. However, there is no difference in the mean of Total-Indirect Impact Ratio (%) between the non-hard-to-abate and hard-to-abate sectors. In fact, the mean for non-hard-to-abate sectors is slightly larger. The transformation of hard-to-abate sectors into more environmentally friendly business models has a knock-on effect on reducing the impact ratio of firms in their supply chains. With a much higher Total-Direct Impact Ratio (%), hard-to-abate sectors have more than double the mean of the Total-Direct + Indirect Impact Ratio (%) compared to non-hard-to-abate sectors. The statistics indicate that hard-to-abate sectors have a much higher Total-direct Impact Ratio (%) on average, but a Total-Indirect Impact Ratio (%) similar to that of non-hard-to-abate sectors.

We modify Eq. (3) with the following specifications to distinguish the environmental risk between the non-hard-to-abate and hard-to-abate sectors:

$$\begin{aligned}\text{CDS}_{it} = \alpha_i + \alpha_{ts} &+ \beta_0 \text{Environmental Impact ratio}_{it} \\ &+ \beta_1 \text{Environmental Impact ratio}_{it} \times I(\text{Speculative-grade}_{it}) \\ &+ \beta_2 \text{Environmental Impact ratio}_{it} \times I(\text{Hard-to-abate}_i) \\ &+ \lambda \text{Controls}_{it} + \epsilon_{it},\end{aligned} \quad (4)$$

where *I(Speculative-grade* $_{it}$*)* equals 1 if, in year t the credit rating for firm i falls into speculative-grade, and *I(hard-to-abate)*$_i$ equals 1 if firm i operates in hard-to-abate sectors. The variables in the specifications remained the same.

Table 6 presents the estimation results of Eq. (4). These results indicate that the environmental risk premium is significantly positive for speculative-grade firms. This

Table 5 CDS spreads and environmental impact ratios by sectors

	Spread (bp)	Total-direct impact ratio (%)	Total-indirect impact ratio (%)	Total-direct + indirect impact ratio (%)
Non-hard-to-abate sectors				
Mean	89.22	0.48	3.00	3.48
Std. dev.	174.65	1.20	5.60	5.88
Hard-to-abate sectors				
Mean	63.36	5.86	2.97	8.82
Std. dev.	85.87	10.10	1.87	10.81

Notes The table reports the mean and standard deviation of CDS spread (bp), Total-Direct Impact Ratio (%), Total-Indirect Impact Ratio (%), and Total-Direct + Indirect Impact Ratio (%) by non-hard-to-abate and hard-to-abate sectors

is consistent with the results in Table 4 in the previous subsection, which show that the environmental risk premium is significantly higher for speculative-grade firms than for investment-grade firms. Additionally, the results also suggest that the coefficient of the interaction term with each corporate environmental impact ratio and the hard-to-abate dummy, β_2, is significantly positive for (1) Total-Direct Impact and insignificant, for (2) Total-Indirect Impact, and (3) Total-Direct + Indirect Impact. This reflects that attention to the hard-to-abate sector focuses mostly on their direct environmental impact, because the reduction in carbon emissions or environmental impact by hard-to-abate sectors contributes to the reduction in the indirect environmental impact of the firms in their supply chain. Their knock-on effects are extensive. Firms operating in hard-to-abate sectors can lower their CDS spreads by mitigating their environmental impact ratios, particularly their direct environmental impacts.

4 CDS Spread Curve and Corporate Environmental Impacts

The results in the previous section focus on the impact of corporate environmental impact ratios on firms' average CDS spreads. This section extends the analysis to the CDS spread curve to investigate whether environmental impact ratios affect the CDS spread curve and to which factor of the CDS spread curve (short-term CDS spread and long-term CDS spread) the environmental impact ratios are priced. The empirical specification is the same as in Eq. (4), but the dependent variable alternates according to which factor of the credit spread term structure we study: short- or long-term CDS spreads.

Table 6 Sectoral impact of environmental impacts of the firm on CDS spreads by credit quality

	Spread		
	(1) Direct	(2) Indirect	(3) Direct + Indirect
Impact ratio	−0.036[b] (0.017)	0.012 (0.009)	0.005 (0.008)
Speculative-grade × Impact ratio	0.006[a] (0.002)	0.010[a] (0.004)	0.006[a] (0.002)
Hard-to-abate × Impact ratio	0.032[c] (0.017)	−0.017 (0.016)	−0.008 (0.008)
AAA rating	−0.051[a] (0.018)	−0.041[b] (0.019)	−0.044[b] (0.018)
AA rating	−0.030 (0.025)	−0.026 (0.026)	−0.025 (0.025)
A rating	−0.006 (0.052)	−0.000 (0.052)	−0.001 (0.052)
Illiquidity	0.033[a] (0.007)	0.033[a] (0.007)	0.033[a] (0.007)
EPS	−0.038[a] (0.011)	−0.037[a] (0.011)	−0.038[a] (0.011)
EBIT margin	0.051 (0.144)	0.048 (0.144)	0.047 (0.144)
Debt/capital	0.186[b] (0.075)	0.184[b] (0.074)	0.185[b] (0.075)
Capex/revenue	−0.378[b] (0.186)	−0.373[b] (0.186)	−0.376[b] (0.186)
ROIC	−0.013 (0.017)	−0.013 (0.017)	−0.012 (0.017)
Price volatility	0.017[a] (0.003)	0.017[a] (0.003)	0.017[a] (0.003)
Year*sector fixed effects	Yes	Yes	Yes
Firm fixed effects	Yes	Yes	Yes
Observations	3215	3215	3215
R^2	0.87	0.87	0.87

Notes The table presents the estimation results of Eq. (4). The credit quality is referred to as investment-grade when the firm's credit rating is above BBB, while the credit quality is referred to as speculative-grade when the firm's credit rating is below BB. Firm fixed effects and year*sector fixed effects are included. Standard errors (SE) clustered at the firm level are in parenthesis. [a] significant at 1%, [b] significant at 5%, [c] significant at 10%

4.1 Environmental Impacts on CDS Curve by Credit Quality

In this subsection, we study the relationship between the corporate environmental impact ratio and short- and long-term CDS spreads. We assume that a short-term CDS spread reflects a firm's urgent credit risk, whereas a long-term CDS spread reflects a firm's credit risk over the long term. Using short- and long-term CDS spreads, we test whether the market regards the corporate environmental impact ratio as an urgent risk or risk of long-term sustainable growth for the firm.

To this end, we estimate a version of Eq. (2) for short-term CDS spreads, which is the average of CDS spreads between six months and four years, and for long-term CDS spreads, which is the average of CDS spreads between five and thirty years. Thus far, the estimation results already indicate that we must control for firm credit quality. Thus, we begin by estimating Eq. (3).

The results in Table 7 confirm that the environmental risk hypothesis (**H1**) is supported by the CDS spreads for speculative-grade firms. This holds for both short- and long-term spreads for all environmental impact ratios: Total-Direct Impact, Total-Indirect Impact, and Total-Direct + Indirect Impact. In contrast, the underreaction hypothesis (**H2**) is supported for investment-grade firms across maturities. This means that lower environmental impact ratios are considered good indicators of firms' sustainability in the speculative-grade credit rating category. However, this impact on CDS spreads is not observed for firms in investment-grade credit categories, partly due to the fact that investment-grade firms are believed to be sustainable already and increasing sustainability further by reducing environmental risk appears to have little impact.

4.2 Environmental Impacts on CDS Curve by Credit Quality and Sector

Finally, we investigate the sectoral impacts on the CDS spread curve by estimating Eq. (4) for short- and long-term CDS spreads. The results in Table 8 generally confirm the findings in the previous subsection for both short- and long-term spreads. Specifically, the environmental risk hypothesis (**H1**) is supported in both the short- and long-term spreads for speculative-grade firms, and the environmental risk premium in the Total-Direct Impact in hard-to-abate sectors is significantly higher than that in non-hard-to-abate sectors in both short- and long-term spreads. Furthermore, the results indicate that the magnitude of the environmental risk premium on the short-term spread is slightly larger. The environmental risk for speculative firms and/or hard-to-abate sector firms is an equally important factor for short- and long-term spreads, but the market perceives that this risk is urgent and expects firms to proceed with the appropriate transition path.

Table 7 CDS spread curve and environmental impact ratio by credit quality

	Short-term spread			Long-term spread		
	(1) Direct	(2) Indirect	(3) Direct + Indirect	(4) Direct	(5) Indirect	(6) Direct + Indirect
Impact ratio	−0.003	0.004	−0.002	−0.003[c]	0.008	−0.002
	(0.003)	(0.009)	(0.003)	(0.002)	(0.007)	(0.002)
Speculative-grade × Impact ratio	0.008[a]	0.012[a]	0.007[a]	0.005[b]	0.011[a]	0.005[a]
	(0.002)	(0.004)	(0.002)	(0.002)	(0.004)	(0.002)
AAA rating	−0.048[b]	−0.039[c]	−0.039[c]	−0.050[a]	−0.039[b]	−0.045[a]
	(0.021)	(0.022)	(0.021)	(0.016)	(0.017)	(0.016)
AA rating	−0.050[c]	−0.045	−0.042	−0.031	−0.025	−0.027
	(0.030)	(0.030)	(0.030)	(0.023)	(0.023)	(0.023)
A rating	−0.023	−0.017	−0.017	−0.016	−0.008	−0.013
	(0.068)	(0.068)	(0.068)	(0.047)	(0.047)	(0.047)
Illiquidity	0.040[a]	0.040[a]	0.040[a]	0.028[a]	0.028[a]	0.028[a]
	(0.010)	(0.010)	(0.010)	(0.006)	(0.006)	(0.006)
EPS	−0.048[a]	−0.047[a]	−0.047[a]	−0.035[a]	−0.034[a]	−0.034[a]
	(0.013)	(0.013)	(0.013)	(0.010)	(0.010)	(0.010)
EBIT margin	0.034	0.032	0.033	0.062	0.062	0.062
	(0.170)	(0.170)	(0.170)	(0.135)	(0.135)	(0.134)
Debt/capital	0.228[b]	0.227[b]	0.228[b]	0.164[b]	0.163[a]	0.164[a]
	(0.093)	(0.092)	(0.093)	(0.064)	(0.063)	(0.064)
Capex/revenue	−0.314	−0.311	−0.314	−0.382[b]	−0.379[b]	−0.381[b]
	(0.232)	(0.232)	(0.232)	(0.157)	(0.157)	(0.157)
ROIC	−0.011	−0.012	−0.011	−0.012	−0.013	−0.012
	(0.022)	(0.021)	(0.022)	(0.016)	(0.015)	(0.015)
Price volatility	0.020[a]	0.020[a]	0.020[a]	0.016[a]	0.015[a]	0.016[a]
	(0.003)	(0.003)	(0.003)	(0.003)	(0.002)	(0.003)
Year*sector fixed effects	Yes	Yes	Yes	Yes	Yes	Yes
Firm fixed effects	Yes	Yes	Yes	Yes	Yes	Yes
Observations	3155	3155	3155	3215	3215	3215
R^2	0.86	0.86	0.86	0.88	0.88	0.88

Notes The table presents the estimation results of Eq. (3) using the short- and long-term CDS spreads as a dependent variable. The first three columns present the effects of corporate environmental impact ratios of Total-Direct Impact Ratio (%), Total-Indirect Impact Ratio (%), and Total-Direct + Indirect Impact Ratio (%) on short-term CDS spreads, while the last three columns present those on long-term CDS spreads. Firm fixed effects and year*sector fixed effects are included. Standard errors (SE) clustered at the firm level are in parenthesis. [a] significant at 1%, [b] significant at 5%, [c] significant at 10%

The results in Tables 7 and 8 suggest that the impact of corporate environmental impact ratios is significant for speculative-grade firms for both short- and long-term CDS spreads. Additionally, the environmental risk premium in the Total-Direct Impact for firms operating in hard-to-abate sectors is substantially larger than that in non-hard-to-abate sectors, regardless of the maturities. This means that corporate environmental risk plays a key role in determining the CDS spread curve for firms

Table 8 CDS spread curve and environmental impact ratio by sector and credit quality

	Short-term spread			Long-term spread		
	(1) Direct	(2) Indirect	(3) Direct + Indirect	(4) Direct	(5) Indirect	(6) Direct + Indirect
Impact ratio	−0.042[b]	0.010	−0.004	−0.031[b]	0.009	0.003
	(0.020)	(0.010)	(0.009)	(0.016)	(0.007)	(0.006)
Speculative-grade × Impact ratio	0.008[a]	0.012[a]	0.007[a]	0.004[b]	0.011[a]	0.005[a]
	(0.002)	(0.004)	(0.002)	(0.002)	(0.004)	(0.002)
Hard-to-abate × Impact ratio	0.040[c]	−0.025	0.001	0.028[c]	−0.009	−0.006
	(0.020)	(0.021)	(0.009)	(0.016)	(0.012)	(0.006)
AAA rating	−0.049[b]	−0.039[c]	−0.039[c]	−0.051[a]	−0.039[b]	−0.044[a]
	(0.021)	(0.022)	(0.021)	(0.016)	(0.017)	(0.016)
AA rating	−0.049	−0.046	−0.042	−0.031	−0.025	−0.026
	(0.030)	(0.030)	(0.030)	(0.023)	(0.023)	(0.023)
A rating	−0.022	−0.016	−0.017	−0.015	−0.008	−0.011
	(0.067)	(0.067)	(0.068)	(0.047)	(0.047)	(0.047)
Illiquidity	0.040[a]	0.040[a]	0.040[a]	0.028[a]	0.028[a]	0.028[a]
	(0.010)	(0.010)	(0.010)	(0.006)	(0.006)	(0.006)
EPS	−0.048[a]	−0.047[a]	−0.047[a]	−0.035[a]	−0.034[a]	−0.034[a]
	(0.013)	(0.013)	(0.013)	(0.010)	(0.010)	(0.010)
EBIT margin	0.037	0.031	0.033	0.064	0.061	0.061
	(0.170)	(0.170)	(0.170)	(0.135)	(0.135)	(0.135)
Debt/capital	0.227[b]	0.226[b]	0.228[b]	0.164[b]	0.163[a]	0.164[a]
	(0.093)	(0.092)	(0.093)	(0.064)	(0.063)	(0.064)
Capex/revenue	−0.316	−0.309	−0.314	−0.383[b]	−0.379[b]	−0.381[b]
	(0.232)	(0.233)	(0.232)	(0.157)	(0.157)	(0.157)
ROIC	−0.012	−0.012	−0.011	−0.013	−0.013	−0.012
	(0.021)	(0.021)	(0.022)	(0.015)	(0.015)	(0.015)
Price volatility	0.021[a]	0.020[a]	0.020[a]	0.016[a]	0.015[a]	0.016[a]
	(0.003)	(0.003)	(0.003)	(0.003)	(0.002)	(0.003)
Year*sector fixed effects	Yes	Yes	Yes	Yes	Yes	Yes
Firm fixed effects	Yes	Yes	Yes	Yes	Yes	Yes
Observations	3155	3155	3155	3215	3215	3215
R^2	0.86	0.86	0.86	0.88	0.88	0.88

Notes The table presents the estimation results of Eq. (4) using the short- and long-term CDS spreads as a dependent variable. The first three columns present the effects of corporate environmental impact ratios of Total-Direct Impact Ratio (%), Total-Indirect Impact Ratio (%), and Total-Direct + Indirect Impact Ratio (%) on short-term CDS spreads, while the last three columns present those on long-term CDS spreads. Firm fixed effects and year*sector fixed effects are included. Standard errors (SE) clustered at the firm level are in parenthesis. [a] significant at 1%, [b] significant at 5%, [c] significant at 10%

exposed to risk, and its effect on the CDS spread curve predicts that it would have a greater impact on a firm's fundraising costs for sustainable growth.

5 Conclusions

This chapter examined the corporate environmental impact ratio in the pricing of firm-level CDS spreads in Japan. First, we found that the underreaction hypothesis (**H2**) is supported in the Japanese CDS market when we do not control for the credit quality of the firm and the sectoral impact. Second, our analysis of CDS spreads supports the environmental risk hypothesis (**H1**) in the CDS spreads for firms in the speculative-grade rating category, regardless of the direct or indirect environmental impact ratio. This means that CDS spreads for firms with smaller environmental impact ratios are lower, as they mitigate their environmental risk. Third, the market or investors focus on the direct environmental impact ratio of firms in hard-to-abate sectors regardless of their credit quality. Finally, corporate environmental impact ratios determine the CDS curve. The results indicate that firms' environmental impact ratios play a key role in the CDS spread curve of the sample firms in Japan.

With more investors seeking action toward net-zero emissions, the firm needs to respond with a strategic plan to mitigate its environmental impact, not only in Japan, but also globally. The results in this chapter imply that higher environmental impact ratios signal a higher risk to a firm's sustainability in the market. This is relevant because the risk of a higher carbon tax and tighter regulation is a global trend, not only in the Asia-Pacific region, but also appears to be irreversible given the active movement toward net-zero emissions. Additionally, the change in end-consumer preferences stemming from the consequences of climate change shifts the demand for greener firms, which leads to downward sales of firms with a high environmental impact. Thus, consumers' awareness of climate risk is directly linked to product sales. Ultimately, firms regarded as not environmentally friendly might suffer from a lack of young people and human resources as the young generation becomes increasingly environmentally conscious. Consequently, more investors consider the sustainable growth of firms with high environmental impacts to be less likely. Our findings from the CDS spread analysis suggest that decarbonization of the hard-to-abate sector is essential not only for itself, but also for its firms in their supply chain, as supply-chain emissions matter in the process of indirect and total environmental impact ratios for any involved firms.

From the viewpoint of accelerating the transition of hard-to-abate sectors, the key implications for policymakers include the need to facilitate and support innovation to decarbonize these sectors. In the Asia-Pacific region, there are traditional and emerging inventive countries for environmental technologies; hence, regional and international policy coordination is required to foster innovation and collaborative activities to boost the transition of hard-to-abate sectors. From the viewpoint of investor responsibility, shifting financial flow through sustainable finance will ultimately benefit society.

Appendix A. Definitions of Variables Used in the Estimations

Variable namel	Unit	Definition
Dependent variable		
CDS_{it}	Basis point	Corporate credit default swap (CDS) spread index at the firm level in year t, which is the arithmetic average of the firm's year-end CDS spreads for its outstanding contracts, following the approach proposed by Gilchrist et al. (2009) and Gilchrist and Zakrajšek (2012) to construct the spread index at the firm level. *Data source*: Markit
Short-term CDS_{it}	Basis point	Corporate credit default swap (CDS) spread index at the firm level in year t, which is the arithmetic average of the firm's year-end CDS spreads for its outstanding contracts between six-month and four-year, *Data source*: Markit
Long-term CDS_{it}	Basis point	Corporate credit default swap (CDS) spread index at the firm level in year t, which is the arithmetic average of the firm's year-end CDS spreads for its outstanding contracts between five- and thirty-years. *Data source*: Markit
Independent variable		
Environment impact ratio		
Direct	%	Total-direct impact ratio (%): Total direct external cost divided by revenue.Direct external environmental impacts are those impacts that a company has on the environment through its own activities. Trucost applies a monetary value to environmental impact quantities, which represents the global average damage of each environmental impact. All values employed are secondary - the synthesis of existing published and unpublished literature. The sum of all the direct external environmental costs of the company is expressed as a percentage of revenue. *Data source*: Trucost

Variable namel	Unit	Definition
Indirect	%	Total-Indirect Impact Ratio (%): Total indirect external cost divided by revenue. All companies have environmental impacts through the goods and services that they purchase, and these are known as supply chain or indirect impacts. Trucost uses advanced environmental modelling to assess a company's indirect environmental impacts. Trucost applies a monetary value to environmental impact quantities, which represents the global average damage of each environmental impact. All values employed are secondary - the synthesis of existing published and unpublished literature. The sum of all the indirect external environmental costs of the company is expressed as a percentage of revenue. *Data source*: Trucost
Direct + Indirect	%	Total-Direct + Indirect Impact Ratio (%): Total direct and indirect external cost divided by revenue. The sum of all the direct and indirect external environmental costs of the company is expressed as a percentage of revenue. *Data source*: Trucost
Firm Controls	*Data source*: Thomson Reuters database	
Credit rating	0/1	A dummy variable for each credit rating category (AAA, AA, A, BBB, BB, B, CCC) which equals 1 when the credit rating for firm i in year t falls into each credit rating category, and equals 0 otherwise
Illiquidity	–	Illiquidity measure explained in Appendix B
EPS	JPY	Earnings Per Share
EBIT margin		Earnings before interest and taxes (EBIT) margin (EBIT/total revenue)
Debt/capital	–	Ratio of debt to capital
Capex/revenue	–	Ratio of capital expenditure (CapEx) to total revenue
ROIC	–	Return on Invested Capital
Price volatility	–	Stock price volatility

Appendix B. Illiquidity Measure

The literature shows that liquidity is a significant factor in corporate bond and CDS spreads. However, unlike stocks, whose trading is centrally organized on stock exchanges, intraday data on quotes and trading volumes are not available to construct the liquidity index. Schestag et al. (2016) provided the comprehensive comparison of common liquidity measures for the US corporate bond market, for example, the ratio of daily high to daily low prices in Roll (1984), Hasbrouck (2009), and Corwin and Schultz (2012). Other measures include the issue size in Campbell and Taksler (2003); bond age in Sarig and Warga (1989), Adams and Mansi (2009), and Mansi et al. (2012); and the number of months a bond is assigned a market quote during the past 12 months in Güntay and Hackbarth (2010). Given the data availability on CDS prices and trading volumes, we constructed a measure of illiquidity based on Bao et al. (2011) which does not require trading volume and intraday bid-ask quotations to construct a measure. This measure is a simple gauge that can be applied to the CDS market, as per Guo and Newton (2013). The details are documented in Bao et al. (2011), and we briefly described how we constructed this measure using CDS data.

The illiquidity measure γ_{it} proposed by Bao et al. (2011) for corporate bonds at time t is used for individual bond issue i. The log price of the asset $lnP_{it} = p_{it}$ is denoted by

$$p_{it} = f_{it} + u_{it}$$

where f_{it} is the fundamental value in the absence of friction and follows a random walk, and u_{it} is transitory and uncorrelated with the fundamental value owing to the impact of illiquidity. The magnitude of u_{it} represents the level of illiquidity. Thus, γ_{it} is used to extract the transitory component from p_{it}. We denote the price change from $t-1$ to t by $\Delta p_{it} = p_{it} - p_{i,t-1}$. The illiquidity measure γ_{it} is defined by the negative autocovariance in relative price changes because transitory price movements result in negatively serially correlated price changes.

We calculated the illiquidity measure γ using daily CDS spread data based on Bao et al. (2011), as follows:

$$\gamma_{it} = cov(\Delta s_t, \Delta s_{i,t+1})$$

where s_{it} is the CDS spread for firm i at time t, that is, the illiquidity measure, γ_{it}, indicates the covariance between daily CDS spread changes. While Bao et al. (2011) denoted the negative autocovariance for corporate bond price changes, we used the positive covariance for the CDS spread, which represents the expected default loss plus credit risk premium (Longstaff et al. (2005)) and whose transitory movements lead to positively serially correlated CDS spread changes. A higher γ value indicates lower liquidity.

We set the horizon over which we measured CDS spread changes across firms to avoid the horizon effect arising from the discrepancy in horizons over which we measured CDS spread changes, and extracted the different aspects of u_{it}. In this section, we used the CDS spread on the year-end trading day in the regressions; therefore, we calculated the illiquidity measure using daily data within a year prior to the last trading day.

References

Acemoglu, D., Aghion, P., Bursztyn, L., and Hemous, D. (2012). The environment and directed technical change. *American Economic Review*, 102(1):131–66.

Acemoglu, D., Akcigit, U., Hanley, D., and Kerr, W. (2018). Transition to clean technology. *Journal of Political Economy*, 124(1):52-104.

Adams, J. C. and Mansi, S. A. (2009). CEO turnover and bondholder wealth. *Journal of Banking & Finance*, 33:522-533.

Aghion, P., Dechezleprêtre, A., Hémous, D., Martin, R., and Van Reenen, J. (2016). Carbon taxes, path dependency, and directed technical change: Evidence from the auto industry. *Journal of Political Economy*, 124(1):1–51.

Bao, J., Pan, J., and Wang, J. (2011). The illiquidity of corporate bonds. *Journal of Finance*, 66(3):911–946.

Barth, F., Hübel, B., and Scholz, H. (2022). ESG and corporate credit spreads. *Journal of Risk Finance*, 23(2):169–190.

Bolton, P. and Kacperczyk, M. (2021a). Do investors care about carbon risk? *Journal of Financial Economics*, 142(2):517–549.

Bolton, P. and Kacperczyk, M. (2021b). The global pricing of carbon-transition risk. NBER Working Paper 28510.

Campbell, J. Y. and Taksler, G. B. (2003). Equity volatility and corporate bond yields. *Journal of Finance*, 58(6):2321–2349.

Cao, J., Li, Y., Zhan, X., Zhang, W., and Zhou, L. (2021). Carbon emissions, institutional trading, and the liquidity of corporate bonds. Working Paper, SSRN eLibrary.

Chava, S. (2014). Environmental externalities and cost of capital. *Management Science*, 60(9):2223-2247.

Colonnello, S., Curatola, G., and Gioffré, A. (2019). Pricing sin stocks: Ethical preference vs. risk aversion. *European Economic Review*, 118:69–100.

Corwin, S. A. and Schultz, P. (2012). A simple way to estimate bid-ask spreads from daily high and low prices. *Journal of Finance*, 67(2):719–759.

Delis, M. D., de Greiff, K., Iosifidi, M., and Ongena, S. (2019). Being stranded the carbon bubble? Climate policy risk and the pricing of bank loans. Swiss Finance Institute Research Paper Series No. 18-10.

Drudi, F., Moench, E., Holthausen, C., Weber, P.-F., Ferrucci, G., Setzer, R., Adao, B., Dées, S., Alogoskoufis, S., and Téllez, M. D. (2021). Climate change and monetary policy in the euro area. Occasional Paper Series 271, European Central Bank.

Duan, T., Li, F. W., and Wen, Q. (2022). Is carbon risk priced in the cross-section of corporate bond returns? *Journal of Financial and Quantitative Analysis*, Forthcoming.

Ehlers, T., Packer, F., and de Greiff, K. (2022). The pricing of carbon risk in syndicated loans: Which risks are priced and why? *Journal of Banking & Finance*, 136:106180.

Fahmy, H. (2022). The rise in investors' awareness of climate risks after the Paris Agreement and the clean energy-oil-technology prices nexus. *Energy Economics*, 106:105738.

Flammer, C. (2021). Corporate green bonds. *Journal of Financial Economics*, 142(2):499–516.

Friedman, M. (1970). The social responsibility of business is to increase its profits. New York Times Magazine, September 13.

Gehde-Trapp, M., Gündüz, Y., and Nasev, J. (2018). The liquidity premium in CDS transaction prices: Do frictions matter? *Journal of Banking & Finance*, 61:184–205.

Gibson, R., Krüger, P., and Mitali, S. F. (2018). The sustainability footprint of institutional investors. European Corporate Governance Institute - Finance Working Paper No. 571/2018.

Gilchrist, S., Yankov, V., and Zakrajšek, E. (2009). Credit market shocks and economic fluctuations: Evidence from corporate bond and stock markets. *Journal of Monetary Economics*, 56(4):471–493.

Gilchrist, S. and Zakrajšek, E. (2012). Credit spreads and business cycle fluctuations. *American Economic Review*, 102(4):1692–1720.

Güntay, L. and Hackbarth, D. (2010). Corporate bond credit spreads and forecast dispersion. *Journal of Banking & Finance*, 34:2328–2345.
Guo, B. and Newton, D. (2013). Regime dependent liquidity determinant of credit default swap spread changes. *Journal of Financial Research*, 36(2):279–298.
Hasbrouck, J. (2009). Trading costs and returns for U.S. equities: Estimating effective costs from daily data. *Journal of Finance*, 64(3):1445–1477.
Haščič, I. and Migotto, M. (2015). Measuring environmental innovation using patent data. OECD Environment Working Papers No. 89.
Heinkel, R., Kraus, A., and Zechner, J. (2001). The effect of green investment on corporate behavior. *Journal of Financial and Quantitative Analysis*, 36(4):431–449.
Hong, H. and Kacperczyk, M. (2009). The price of sin: The effects of social norms on markets. *Journal of Financial Economics*, 93(1):15–36.
Hsu, P.-H., Li, K., and Tsou, C.-Y. (2019). The pollution premium. Working Paper.
Huynh, T. D. and Xia, Y. (2021). Climate change news risk and corporate bond returns. *Journal of Financial and Quantitative Analysis*, 56(6):1985–2009.
Ilhan, E., Sautner, Z., and Vilkov, G. (2021). Carbon tail risk. *Review of Financial Studies*, 34(3):1540–1571.
In, S. Y., Park, K. Y., and Monk, A. (2010). Is 'being green' rewarded in the market?: An empirical investigation of decarbonization and stock returns. Stanford Global Project Center Working Paper.
Jang, G.-Y., Kang, H.-G., Lee, J.-Y., and Bae, K. (2020). ESG scores and the credit market. *Sustainability*, 12(8):1–13.
Kacperczyk, M. T. and Peydro, J. (2022). Carbon emissions and the bank-lending channel. Working Paper, SSRN eLibrary.
Kölbel, J. F., Leippold, M., Rillaerts, J., and Wang, Q. (2022). Ask BERT: How regulatory disclosure of transition and physical climate risks affects the CDS term structure. *Journal of Financial Econometrics*, page nbac027.
Krueger, P., Sautner, Z., and Starks, L. T. (2020). The importance of climate risks for institutional investors. *Review of Financial Studies*, 33(3):1067–1111.
Longstaff, F. A., Mithal, S., and Neis, E. (2005). Corporate yield spreads: Default risk or liquidity? New evidence from the credit default swap market. *Journal of Finance*, 60(5):2213–2253.
Luo, H. A. and Balvers, R. J. (2017). Social screens and systematic investor boycott risk. *Journal of Financial and Quantitative Analysis*, 52(1):365–399.
Mansi, S. A., Maxwell, W. F., and Zhang, A. (2012). Bankruptcy prediction models and the cost of debt. *Journal of Fixed Income*, 21(4):25–42.
OECD (2019). *The Costs of Decarbonisation: System Costs with High Shares of Nuclear and Renewables*. Nuclear Energy Agency, OECD Publishing, OECD Paris.
Oestreich, A. M. and Tsiakas, I. (2015). Carbon emissions and stock returns: Evidence from the EU emissions trading scheme. *Journal of Banking & Finance*, 58:294–308.
Okimoto, T. and Takaoka, S. (2024). Sustainability and credit spreads in Japan. *International Review of Financial Analysis, 91*, 103052.
Pastor, L., Stambaugh, R. F., and Taylor, L. A. (2021). Sustainable investing in equilibrium. *Journal of Financial Economics*.
Pedersen, L. H., Fitzgibbons, S., and Pomorski, L. (2021). Responsible investing: The ESG-efficient frontier. *Journal of Financial Economics*, 142(2):572–597.
Roll, R. (1984). A simple implicit measure of the effective bid-ask spread in an efficient market. *Journal of Finance*, 39(4):1127–1139.
Sarig, O. and Warga, A. (1989). Bond price data and bond market liquidity. *Journal of Financial and Quantitative Analysis*, 24(3):367–378.
Schestag, R., Schuster, P., and Uhrig-Homburg, M. (2016). Measuring liquidity in bond markets. *Review of Financial Studies*, 29(5):1170–1219.
Stellner, C., Klein, C., and Zwergel, B. (2015). Corporate social responsibility and Eurozone corporate bonds: The moderating role of country sustainability. *Journal of Banking and Finance*, 59:538 – 549.

Stroebel, J. and Wurgler, J. (2021). What do you think about climate finance? *Journal of Financial Economics*, 142(2):487–498.

Teske, S., Niklas, S., Atherton, A., Kelly, S., and Herring, J. (2020). Sectoral pathways to net zero emissions. Report prepared by the University of Technology Sydney for the Net Zero Asset Owners Alliance.

The Energy Transitions Commission (2018). Mission possible: Reaching net-zero carbon emissions from harder-to-abate sectors. November 2018.

Zerbib, O. D. (2019). The effect of pro-environmental preferences on bond prices: Evidence from green bonds. *Journal of Banking and Finance*, 98:39–60.

Zerbib, O. D. (2022). A sustainable capital asset pricing model (S-CAPM): Evidence from environmental integration and sin stock exclusion. Proceedings of Paris December 2020 Finance Meeting EUROFIDAI - ESSEC.

Greenhouse Gas Emissions and Loan Markets in Japan

Koji Takahashi and Junnosuke Shino

1 Introduction

This chapter investigates whether banks consider a firm's greenhouse gas (GHG) emissions in their lending decisions, using Japan as a case study. In today's financial market, firms' environmental, social, and governance (ESG) performance has gained in importance as social awareness has increased. In particular, many investors today consider climate risk, included in the "environment" category, an important factor in investment decisions. In parallel, to address environmental concerns, policymakers, such as the European Central Bank and the Bank of Japan (BOJ), have embarked on initiatives under the rubric of "green" monetary policies. For example, in 2021, the BOJ introduced "Climate Response Financing Operations," to provide long-term funds with a zero percent lending rate to eligible "green" investments, such as green loans/bonds, sustainability-linked loans/bonds, and transition finance.[1]

However, efforts to deal with climate risk have not been limited to such "green" initiatives. Central banks and financial regulatory agencies have begun to integrate climate stress testing into their supervisory frameworks. This approach involves assessing the impact of climate-related risks on financial institutions and the broader

[1] For more detail, see, for example, https://www.boj.or.jp/en/mopo/measures/mkt_ope/ope_x/index.htm.

The views expressed in this paper are those of the authors and do not necessarily reflect the official views of the Bank for International Settlements.

K. Takahashi (✉)
Bank for International Settlements, Basel, Switzerland
e-mail: koji.takahashi@bis.org

J. Shino
Waseda University, Tokyo, Japan
e-mail: junnosuke.shino@waseda.jp

S. Takaoka (ed.), *Environmental Technology Innovation and ESG Investment*,
https://doi.org/10.1007/978-981-99-9768-8_4

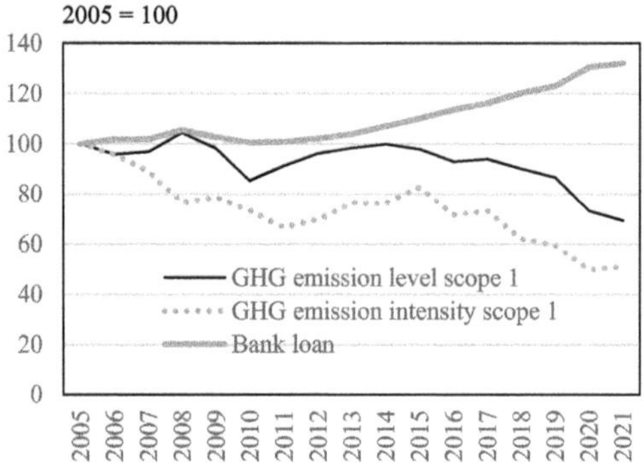

Fig. 1 GHG emissions and bank loans in Japan. *Note* The figure shows GHG emissions and intensity for Scope 1 and total bank loans to private firms in Japan standardized with 2005 values. GHG emissions and intensity are calculated using the weighted average of the change rates for firms whose data are available for two consecutive years at each point in time. As for the definition of Scope 1, see Sect. 2.1. *Sources* Trucost, Bank of Japan

economy. Their aim is to enhance transparency, resilience, and preparedness in the face of a changing climate.

From a long-term perspective, Japanese firms have been pursuing energy efficiency for more than 30 years. As shown in Fig. 1, a discernible decline in the magnitude of energy efficiency has been evident since the latter half of the 2000s.

To ensure a deeper understanding of the effects of green monetary policy, policymakers need to be able to discern the intricate interplay between the conduct of financial intermediaries and climate risk. From this perspective, banks have the potential to affect borrowing firm behavior through their credit allocation policies. Thus, a substantial body of literature has delved into the relationship between climate risk and bank lending. The literature finds that firms with higher ESG scores or lower GHG emissions tend to incur lower borrowing costs. However, investments of financial institutions are not only expected to reflect firm exposure to climate risk but also confront mounting pressure to curtail investment in firms that undermine the environment. Put differently, the allocation of credit to enterprises characterized as environmentally conscientious (commonly referred to as "green") and those that lack such credentials (commonly known as "brown") is at the epicenter of policy deliberations.

In the context of our study, we should note that identifying the relationship between bank loans and GHG emissions is neither simple nor easy, as many factors, such as energy policy and macroeconomic conditions, influence GHG emissions and bank loans in various ways. To illustrate this, we show in Fig. 1 the evolution of both the bank loans to private firms and the GHG emission variables (level and intensity) in Japan from 2005 to 2021. As we can see in the figure, after the 2010s, bank loans to private firms follow a steady upward trend. However, the intensity of GHG emissions, which decreases in the 2000s, increases again after 2011, partly reflecting the temporary shutdown of nuclear power plants due to the 2011 earthquake. Subsequently, these emissions decline again in the late 2010s. Thus, there is no clear relationship between loan growth rates and GHG emissions, reflecting the limitations of trying to analyze this relationship based solely on these aggregate variables. In other words, we need to control macroeconomic factors to better understand the nexus between GHG emissions and bank loans. In this chapter, we investigate bank–firm level data to disentangle different factors by focusing on supply-side effects.

There is an expanding body of literature examining the intricate relationship between credit instruments, climate risk, and ESG scores. Ehlers et al. (2022) identify a "carbon premium" in syndicated loans after the Paris Agreement, finding a modest impact. Ongena et al. (2018) show that loans to firms with higher fossil reserves incur higher interest rates, while Kleimeier and Viehs (2018) find that increased carbon emissions positively and significantly affect loan spreads.

Furthermore, several studies highlight that firms with higher ESG scores tend to have lower credit risk (Sharfman and Fernando 2008; Goss and Roberts 2011; Chava 2014; Ge and Liu 2015; Hasan et al. 2017; Hauptmann 2017). Scatigna et al. (2021) examine the risk premium of corporate bonds for firms with higher GHG emissions, revealing that these firms also bear greater default risk, albeit marginally. Regarding analyses of green bonds, that is, bonds whose proceeds are used to finance environmental and climate-friendly projects, Flammer (2021) shows that the announcement of a green bond issuance positively influences the abnormal stock returns of the issuing company. The issuing company then tends to improve its environmental performance, such as through higher environmental ratings and lower CO_2 emissions. Zerbib (2019) compares each green bond with an otherwise identical counterfactual conventional bond and argues that the yield of the green bond is lower than that of the conventional bond, reflecting investors' pro-environmental preferences.

Our research closely aligns with Houston and Shan's (2022) exploration of the interplay between firm ESG scores and bank lending. They find that banks tend to increase their lending to firms with higher ESG scores; at the same time, notably, firms borrowing from banks with superior ESG scores are more likely to have higher ESG ratings than those borrowing from institutions with lower ESG scores. Reghezza et al. (2022) also investigate the impact of GHG emissions on bank loans, focusing on the Paris Agreement. They argue that highly polluting firms receive reduced credit allocations thereafter. Kacperczyk et al. (2021) look at banks' commitments to carbon neutrality and syndicate loan data for global firms, discovering that such bank commitments lead to fewer loans to firms with higher GHG emissions. Benincasa et al. (2022) investigate the effect of stringent climate policies on cross-border lending using syndicated loan data and find evidence of regulatory arbitrage.

A substantial body of the literature also scrutinizes the correlation between stock prices and climate risk. Bolton et al. (2021) reveal that firms with higher carbon dioxide emissions often yield greater returns on their stocks, suggesting that investors seek compensation for their exposure to GHG emissions risk. In et al. (2017) examine a portfolio consisting of long stocks of firms with low GHG emissions and short stocks of those with high GHG emissions and conclude that the portfolio generates positive abnormal returns. Aswani et al. (2023), in contrast, argue that the results in

Bolton et al. (2021) weaken or disappear when differences between vendor estimated emissions and firm disclosed emissions are accounted for.

Ultimately, our study extends the Japanese literature on firm performance and GHG emissions. Among such studies, Aruga et al. (2022) conclude that firms with lower GHG emissions tend to exhibit superior performance and incur lower capital costs. Most notably, Nishitani et al. (2012) and Fujii et al. (2013) use Japanese firm data from 2006 to 2008 to demonstrate that lower GHG emissions positively influence firm performance. Shirasu and Kawakita (2021) investigate the relationship between corporate social responsibility (CSR) and long-term stock performance. They conclude that CSR activities are positively related to long-term stock returns, while short-term CSR investment does not yield strong stock performance. Regarding credit instruments in Japan and ESG, Okimoto and Takaoka (2021) find that elevated ESG scores result in decreased spreads for corporate bonds.

Our aim here is to investigate the impact of firm GHG emissions on bank lending behavior in Japan by using bank–firm level data to disentangle various macro factors. The rest of the chapter is organized as follows. Section 2 presents our methodology covering our dataset and how we identify the developments in GHG emissions in Japanese firms since the 2000s. Section 3 presents our results which detail the relationship between bank loans and GHG emissions using firm- and bank-fixed effects panel regressions (Sect. 3.1). This section also attempts to identify the dominant factors that influence the identified relationship, namely, brown- or non-brown sectors (Sect. 3.2), major or small banks (Sect. 3.3), and demand or supply (Sect. 3.4) and extends the scope to non-banking institutions in the banking sector (Sect. 3.5). Finally, Sect. 4 concludes and identifies topics for future research.

2 Methodology

2.1 Data

We combine two comprehensive datasets to examine the impact of GHG emissions on bank loans while accounting for other influential factors. First, for GHG emissions, we use firm-level data sourced from Trucost. Next, we merge these figures with loan data extracted from Nikkei NEEDS FinancialQuest, pertaining specifically to publicly listed Japanese firms. Finally, we incorporate pertinent financial variables concerning both banks and firms from the Nikkei NEEDS databse. The investigation encompasses annual data spanning 2006 to 2022.

Regarding GHG emission metrics, we distinguish three distinct categories: Scope 1, Scope 2, and Scope 3 emissions. According to Trucost (2018), Scope 1 emissions encapsulate those that stem directly from sources under a company's direct control. For instance, this would encompass emissions generated by an in-house fleet of lorries owned by a transportation company. Scope 2 emissions pertain to those arising from the consumption of externally procured electricity or other forms of energy originating upstream from a company's direct operations. Scope 3 encompasses all other emissions tied to a company's operations that are not directly owned or controlled by the company. In our ensuing empirical examination, we scrutinize the impact of GHG emissions on bank loans, focusing on GHG emissions under Scope 1. This is partly because previous studies find that Scope 1 is the most strongly associated with firm valuations, including stock returns and credit spreads, and partly because the measurement errors of Scope 2 and 3 could be relatively large compared with those for Scope 1. Specifically, following Bolton and Kacperczyk (2021) and Garvey et al. (2018), we consider both the raw Scope 1 GHG emissions level and the ratio of the Scope 1 emissions level to sales, denoted as emission intensity. These measures are labeled GEGL and GEGI, respectively.

Table 1 provides a concise overview of the summary statistics of the variables in our study. Throughout the sample period, the average loan growth rate is positive, yet the median growth rate remains at zero percentage points. The dataset for loan growth rates encompasses more than 30,000 observations. However, GHG emissions data comprise about 4,900 firm-year samples. Notably, Scope 1 GHG emissions exhibit greater variability. Return on assets (ROA) for the firms in our sample is a positive value of 2.7%. For bank variables, we have approximately 1,500 bank-year samples, indicating that the number of banks in our sample hovers around 100 annually.

Table 1 Summary statistics

Variable	Median	Mean	Std. Dev.	Min.	Max.	N
Loan growth rates (%)	0	10.6	63.0	−78.2	566.6	31,556
Firm variables						
Firm leverage (%)	52.0	52.4	17.4	4.6	116.7	4964
Firm return on assets (%)	2.7	3.1	3.8	−11.9	14.2	4964
Firm size (log(total assets))	12.0	11.9	1.5	6.8	16.3	4964
GHG emission scope 1 (thousand tons)	39	908	4897	15	93,079	4964
GHG emission intensity scope 1	22.9	143.3	543.8	0.01	8983	3677
Bank variables						
Bank book leverage (%)	94.8	94.8	1.6	87.2	99.6	1543
Bank return on assets (%)	0.2	0.2	0.2	−0.4	0.9	1543
Bank size (log(total assets))	14.9	15.1	1.2	12.3	19.4	1543

Note The table indicates descriptive statistics for firms and banks with loan data

Table 2 Number of firms in the sample by sector

Sector	Number of firms
Energy	11
Materials	116
Capital goods	208
Commercial and professional services	38
Transportation	39
Automobiles and components	59
Consumer durables and apparel	56
Consumer services	44
Consumer discretionary distribution and retail	58
Consumer staples distribution and retail	25
Food, beverage and tobacco	40
Household and personal products	11
Health care equipment and services	26
Pharmaceuticals, biotechnology and life sciences	15
Financial services	16
Software and services	36
Technology hardware and equipment	63
Semiconductors and semiconductor equipment	22
Telecommunication services	3
Media and entertainment	10
Utilities	9
Real estate	72
Total	977

Note This table presents the descriptive statistics for firms with loan data to be used in the regression analysis

Table 2 presents the number of firms in the sample by sector. Although the capital goods sector represents the largest number of firms, our data cover a wide range of sectors, including the service sector. Thus, our analysis provides a comprehensive picture of the relationship between bank loans and GHG emissions for Japanese listed firms.

2.2 *Identifying GHG Emissions Development in Japanese Firms*

Before examining the relationship between bank loans and GHG emissions in more depth, we identify the basic features of GHG emissions in Japanese firms. First, in

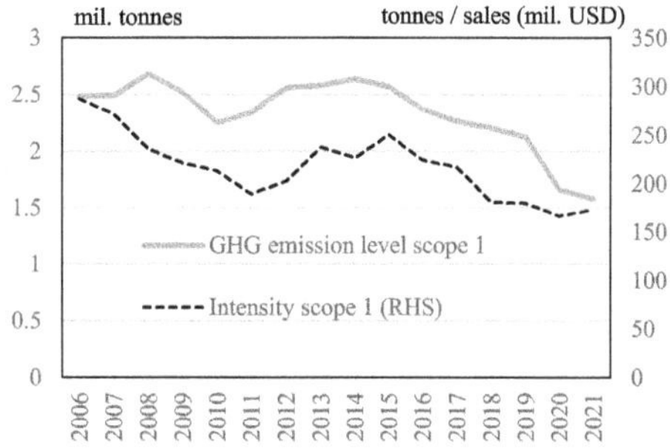

Fig. 2 GHG emission level and intensity. *Note* Average yearly GHG emissions level and intensity for Japanese firms with available data for the entire sample period from 2006 to 2021. *Source* Trucost

Fig. 2, we show the development of GHG emissions considering our sample. Thus, in the figure, we show only the firms with available GHG emissions data for the entire sample period from 2006 to 2021. The trend in Fig. 2 is similar to that in Fig. 1, where all the available samples are used. Specifically, after the global financial crisis, GHG emissions decline as the economy slows. However, after 2011, emissions start to increase again, owing to the Japan government reconsidering its energy policy after the Tohoku earthquake. Following that, partly because the nuclear power plants start operating again, GHG emissions decline. Emission intensity shows a similar pattern, although it is less affected by the earthquake and declines during the sample period. The figure confirms that the decline in GHG emissions and intensity is not driven by restricting the firms in the analysis.

Although we show that the GHG emissions and intensity of Japanese firms decline over time, it is well known that the heterogeneity across sectors is substantial. Table 3 shows the GHG emission levels by sector. The average GHG emissions in the energy and utilities, materials, and transportation sectors are substantially higher than those in other sectors. Although emissions increase in the 2010s because the operations of nuclear power plants stop, they show a decreasing trend in the sample period as a whole. Although the level is low, in manufacturing sectors, such as capital goods, and automobiles and components, GHG emissions decline substantially by more than 20%. In contrast, the semiconductor sector shows an increase in emissions. However, we need to account for the fact that the number of observations is small in that sector.

Table 4 shows the average GHG emission intensity measured in tons per sale (mil. USD). The energy and utility sectors have the highest GHG emission intensity, in line with their emission levels. Similarly, the transportation and materials sectors show high intensity. For almost all sectors except diversified financial services, the intensity decreases in 2021 compared with 2006. For example, the intensity of the software and service sectors decrease by 20%, even though the emissions level doubled.

As shown in Tables 3 and 4, energy efficiency in terms of GHG emission intensity improves in almost all sectors; although the GHG emission level shows more variation across sectors, reflecting the energy mix change after the Tohoku earthquake.

Table 3 GHG scope 1 emissions by sector

	2006	2011	2016	2021	Number of firms
Energy and utilities	2,14,74,603	1,80,76,954	2,09,13,170	1,12,76,046	9
Materials	57,20,175	58,11,737	51,23,918	53,44,561	40
Capital goods	7,69,195	10,42,300	9,18,218	5,78,886	53
Transportation	21,50,240	28,24,721	23,81,593	12,72,533	18
Automobiles and components	6,20,611	5,57,345	5,10,548	4,58,965	21
Consumer durables and apparel	2,91,919	2,14,574	1,50,151	1,28,597	23
Consumer discretionary distribution and retail	55,623	70,547	55,724	45,284	12
Consumer staples distribution and retail	1,22,900	1,56,095	1,51,544	94,454	6
Food, beverage and tobacco	3,28,831	3,11,589	2,47,580	2,42,016	19
Health care equipment and services	2,15,742	3,45,452	1,72,167	1,77,637	6
Pharmaceuticals, biotechnology and life sciences	1,32,758	1,56,490	56,494	63,434	12
Banks	8,180	7,582	8,338	5,734	16
Diversified financial service	17,210	40,412	43,878	1,43,905	7
Software and services	25,404	63,906	41,047	57,068	12
Technology hardware and equipment	3,48,788	2,37,697	1,74,633	1,70,490	29
Semiconductors and semiconductor equipment	1,04,073	1,58,494	60,862	1,13,655	5
Real estate	74,562	77,080	5,99,020	30,331	8

Note The table shows the simple average GHG emissions for Scope 1 by sector across firms with available data during the entire sample period (2006–2021), indicated in tons. We exclude sectors with fewer than five firms for the entire sample period. *Source* Trucost

Table 4 Intensity scope 1 by sector

	2006	2011	2016	2021
Energy and utilities	1,356	762	1,038	595
Materials	924	627	669	681
Capital goods	81	74	68	37
Transportation	286	267	263	194
Automobiles and components	23	16	13	13
Consumer durables and apparel	27	14	12	10
Consumer discretionary distribution and retail	17	12	10	7
Consumer staples distribution and retail	10	7	6	4
Food, beverage and tobacco	66	39	37	33
Household and personal products	121	120	173	24
Health care equipment and services	25	22	12	12
Pharmaceuticals, biotechnology and life sciences	36	26	11	9
Banks	1	1	1	1
Diversified financial service	3	6	6	18
Software and services	10	13	10	8
Technology hardware and equipment	27	14	13	14
Semiconductors and semiconductor equipment	31	28	19	20
Real estate	27	17	152	7

Note The table shows the average GHG emission intensity for Scope 1 by sector across firms with available data during the entire sample period (2006–2021), indicated as tons per sales (million USD). *Source* Trucost

3 Results: Bank Loans and GHG Emissions

3.1 Baseline Results

In this section, we analyze bank–firm-level data. To present a rough picture of the relationships, in Fig. 3, we plot the loan growth rates at the bank–firm level and the borrowing firms' GHG emissions for Scope 1. We can see a negative relationship between the two. On average, higher firm GHG emissions are associated with lower bank loan growth rates.

As discussed, loan growth rates are affected by many factors, such as macroeconomic fluctuations and financial market conditions. Therefore, one might argue that the loan growth rate could correlate with GHG emissions through factors such as business cycles. To control these effects, we run a panel regression for a loan to firm i from bank j as follows:

$$\Delta Loan_{ijt} = \gamma_j + \beta GHG_{it-1} + Control_{ijt} + Time_t + \epsilon_{ijt}, \tag{1}$$

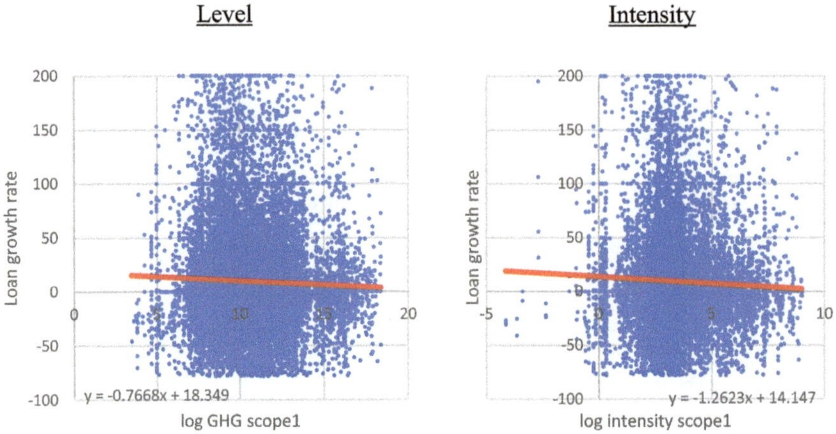

Fig. 3 Loan growth rates and GHG emissions. *Notes* This figure shows a scatter plot of the growth rate of loans at the bank–firm level and the log of GHG emission variables. *Source* Trucost, Nikkei NEEDS Financial Quest

where GHG_{it-1} is the GHG emissions variable for firm *i*. We should note that banks will evaluate emission levels based on certain criteria. We use the average emissions variable as a proxy for this. Specifically, we use the deviation of the GHG emissions level (GHGL) and intensity (GHGI) from the average across firms in each year. Specifically, we use the residual obtained from a regression ($devi_{it}$), where we regress the GHG emissions variable on time dummies as follows:

$$GHG_{it} = TimeDummy_t + devi_{it}.$$

In addition, to address the endogeneity problem, we incorporate a lag of one period for the GHG emissions variables. As control variables, we include the one-period lagged book leverage ratio (Book Lev), return on assets (ROA), and the log of total assets (Size) of banks and firms. γ_j indicates the bank fixed effect. In this analysis, we do not include firm or sector fixed effects. In other words, our specification can exploit the variations across different sectors and allow us to investigate the allocation effect of GHG emissions across different sectors.

Our results are presented in Table 5. The deviation from the average GHG emissions has a significantly negative coefficient, as shown in column (1), indicating that loans to firms with higher GHG emissions are more likely to decrease than those to firms with lower GHG emissions. The impact is economically significant; that is, the 75 and 25 percentiles are 1.35 and -1.66, respectively, as shown in Table 6. The average and median impact is small partly by construction, but the results show that the impact varies substantially across loans. Takahashi and Shino (2023) show that these results are robust even when we control time-varying bank and sector fixed effects, as well as other firm variables.

Table 5 Impact of GHG emission level and intensity on loan growth rates

	(1)	(2)
	Δ LOAN	Δ LOAN
GHGL	−1.209*** (0.285)	
GHGI		−1.426*** (0.374)
Bank book lev	0.668 (0.678)	0.638 (0.867)
Bank ROA	0.898 (3.559)	0.814 (3.507)
Bank size	−0.775 (1.933)	−0.998 (2.429)
Firm book lev	−0.0311 (0.0459)	−0.0436 (0.0522)
Firm ROA	0.414* (0.215)	0.371 (0.230)
Firm size	0.747 (0.429)	0.0279 (0.532)
N	31,104	30,001
R^2	0.016	0.015
Bank fixed effects	Yes	Yes
Year fixed effects	Yes	Yes

Note: * $p < 0.10$, ** $p < 0.05$, *** $p < 0.01$. Results for the panel regression in Eq. (1). Clustered standard errors at the year and bank levels are presented in parentheses

Table 6 Impact of GHG emissions on loan growth rate

10 percentile	25 percentile	50 percentile	75 percentile	90 percentile
−3.58	−1.66	−0.14	1.35	2.78

Note This table indicates the distribution of the impact on loan growth rates as percentage points, which are calculated using the estimated coefficients and the observed deviation of the GHG emission level from the yearly average

The deviation in GHG emission intensity also has a significantly negative coefficient, as shown in column (2) of Table 5, which indicates that higher GHG intensity is associated with lower bank loan growth rates to high emitters. This implies that banks are decreasing their loans to firms with higher GHG emissions and intensity.

3.2 Brown Sectors and Loan Lending

In the previous section, we show that loans to higher GHG emitters decrease more than those to low emitters. However, as discussed, there is a significant variation in Scope 1 GHG emissions across sectors. GHG emissions are particularly high in the energy, utilities, materials, and transportation sectors. As those sectors are recognized as "brown" sectors, bank lending behavior could differ for loans to firms in these sectors. For example, banks could be paying attention to GHG emissions only in these sectors and providing loans in non-brown sectors without such consideration. To investigate the difference between brown and non-brown sectors, we estimate a panel regression by adding an interaction term with a brown sector firm dummy. Specifically, the brown sector dummy takes one if the firm is included in one of the energy, utilities, materials, and transportation sectors based on the GICS standard, and zero otherwise. The estimation regression is as follows:

$$\Delta Loan_{ijt} = \gamma_j + \beta_0 GHG_{it-1} + \beta_1 GHG_{it-1} * BrownDummy_i + Control_{ijt} + Time_t + \epsilon_{ijt}.$$

The results shown in Table 7 indicate that the interaction effect between GHG emissions and the brown sector dummy is insignificantly different from zero, albeit positive. In addition, the brown sector dummy is estimated to be significantly negative. This implies that loans to firms in brown sectors tend to decrease more than those in non-brown sectors, on average. However, we find no additional effect of the GHG emission variables on loans to firms in the brown sector. In other words, because the GHG emission variable has a negative coefficient, it has an effect on all loans, even those in non-brown sectors. We obtain a similar result when we use GHG emission intensity, as shown in column (2) of Table 7. This suggests that the GHG emission variables are important determinants of lending in a wide range of sectors.

3.3 Major Banks and Small Banks

Thus far, we have confirmed that GHG emissions are associated with bank loans' low growth rates. If this effect of GHG emissions arises mainly from bank-side factors, it would differ across banks depending on their characteristics. Accordingly, we focus on the differences between major and non-major banks. We define major banks as large banks headquartered in metropolitan cities. These major banks have played an important role in the Japanese economy, as discussed in Hoshi and Kashyap (1999). Notably, the average balance sheet size of major banks, as measured by total assets, is much larger (86.8 trillion yen as of 2020) than that of non-major banks (6.9 trillion yen).

Table 7 Brown sectors and GHG emission effect

	(1)	(2)
	Δ LOAN	Δ LOAN
GHGL	−1.261** (0.471)	
Brown dummy x GHGL	1.360 (0.827)	
GHGI		−1.170** (0.471)
Brown dummy x GHGI		0.860 (1.005)
Brown dummy	−4.577** (1.700)	−4.005* (2.028)
N	31,104	30,001
R^2	0.016	0.016
Firm controls	Yes	Yes
Bank controls	Yes	Yes
Year fixed effect	Yes	Yes
Bank fixed effect	Yes	Yes

Note * $p < 0.10$, ** $p < 0.05$, *** $p < 0.01$. Results for panel regression with loan growth rates as the dependent variable. Clustered standard errors at the year and bank levels are presented in parentheses

To investigate the heterogeneous effect, we include the interaction effect between the GHG emission variables and the major bank dummy as follows:

$$\begin{aligned}\Delta Loan_{ijt} = \gamma_j + \beta_0 GHG_{it-1} + \beta_1 GHG_{it-1} \times Major_j \\ + Control_{ijt} + Time_t + \epsilon_{ijt}\end{aligned} \tag{2}$$

where $Major_j$ takes the value of one if bank j is a major bank, and zero otherwise. Our variable of interest is β_1, which shows an additional effect for loans provided by major banks. If the major banks are more conservative in loans to high emitters, then the coefficient will be negative. The results are reported in Table 8. The interaction effect with the major bank dummy is not statistically significant, which means that both major and non-major banks are sensitive to borrowers' GHG emission levels and intensity in the same magnitude. In our earlier study, we investigate more extensively the heterogeneous effects across banks (Takahashi and Shino 2023).

Table 8 Heterogenous effects for major banks

	(1) Δ LOAN	(2) Δ LOAN
GHGL	−1.083*** (0.339)	
MAJOR x GHGL	−0.253 (0.465)	
GHGI		−1.339*** (0.434)
MAJOR x GHGI		−0.125 (0.456)
N	31097	29995
R^2	0.016	0.015
Firm controls	Yes	Yes
Bank controls	Yes	Yes
Bank fixed effects	Yes	Yes
Year fixed effects	Yes	Yes

Note * $p < 0.10$, ** $p < 0.05$, *** $p < 0.01$. Results for the panel regression in Eq. (2). Clustered standard errors at the year and bank levels are presented in parentheses

3.4 Demand and Supply Effects

In the previous section, we discuss the negative relationship between the loan growth rate and borrowers' GHG emissions. These results can be interpreted in two ways. The first is the demand-side view, where firms with higher GHG emissions may have less demand for loan funding. The other is the supply-side view, which implies that banks avoid lending to firms with higher emissions. To investigate which view is more plausible in explaining the relationship between GHG emissions and loans, we estimate the panel regression limiting our sample to loans for firms expected to have some funding demand, following Becker and Ivashina (2014). If firms have funding demands and GHG emissions have a negative impact on the loan growth rate, the effect is most likely driven by supply-side factors. Specifically, we use samples only for firms whose total debt increased from the previous year. These firms are likely to need debt funding, and thus a demand for loans.

Table 9 shows the results, indicating that high GHG emissions are associated with lower loan growth rates, even when we use samples with high funding demand. The results are robust for both GHG emission level and intensity. This suggests that the effects of the GHG emission variables on bank loans are not driven by demand factors. Instead, the finding suggests that banks avoid lending to high-emitter or low-efficiency firms considering GHG emission intensity.

We also review the relationship between a proxy for firm funding demand and GHG emissions. Specifically, we examine how GHG emissions relate to firm sales growth rates. We control the effects of the firm-side variables as follows:

$$\text{Sales}\,Growth_{it} = \beta_0 GHG_{it-1} + \beta_1 Control_{it} + YearFE_t + e_{it}$$

Table 9 Effect of GHG emissions for firms with funding demand

	(1) Δ LOAN	(2) Δ LOAN
GHGL	−0.952* (0.451)	
GHGI		−1.073* (0.592)
N	18,874	18,149
R^2	0.020	0.020
Firm controls	Yes	Yes
Bank controls	Yes	Yes
Bank fixed effects	Yes	Yes
Year fixed effects	Yes	Yes

Note * $p < 0.10$, ** $p < 0.05$, *** $p < 0.01$. The results for the panel regression in Eq. (1) looking at borrowing firms with increased total debt from the previous year. Clustered standard errors at the year and bank levels are presented in parentheses

If the GHG emissions are associated with low demand from the firm side, β_0 is expected to be significantly negative. However, as shown in Table 10, the GHG emission coefficients are not significantly different from zero, suggesting that high GHG emissions are not associated with lower funding demand.

Table 10 Sales growth and GHG emissions

	(1) Sales growth	(2) Sales growth
GHGL	−0.602 (0.379)	
GHGI		−0.315 (0.342)
Firm book lev	−0.00919 (0.0324)	−0.0121 (0.0315)
Firm ROA	0.247 (0.178)	0.248 (0.175)
Firm size	−0.368 (0.280)	−0.806*** (0.258)
N	3862	3862
R^2	0.084	0.081
Firm fixed effects	Yes	Yes
Year fixed effects	Yes	Yes

Note * $p < 0.10$, ** $p < 0.05$, *** $p < 0.01$. The results for the panel regression use firm sales growth as the dependent variable. Clustered standard errors at the year and firm levels are shown in parentheses

3.5 Non-bank Financial Institutions: Insurance Companies

Using the same database source, we extend our analysis by investigating the relationship between loans provided by insurance companies and borrowers' GHG emissions. To the best of our knowledge, ours is the first study to investigate loans provided by Japanese insurance companies and GHG emissions. Recently, the role of non-bank financial institutions in financial markets, including capital allocation, has garnered increasing attention from policymakers and market participants (IMF, 2023). Although loans from Japanese insurance companies to non-financial firms have been gradually decreasing, especially in the early 2000s, they still represent a substantial outstanding amount, as shown in Fig. 4. Furthermore, insurance companies have a longer investment horizon under asset liability management, as their liabilities have a longer duration. This extended investment horizon could lead to greater consideration of the long-term environmental effects of their investments. In other words, insurance companies may be more sensitive to the GHG emissions of the borrowing firms than banks are.

To assess this, we use insurance company loan data from the Nikkei NEEDS FinancialQuest database. While the bank loan data cover approximately 100 banks, the insurance company loan data include only 26 insurance companies.

The results shown in Table 11 indicate that the GHG emission level has a significantly negative coefficient, while the coefficient on intensity is not significantly different from zero. This implies that loans from insurance companies are affected by GHG emissions, although the magnitude of the impact is slightly smaller than that of loans from banks (Table 5). One possible explanation for the smaller impact could be that insurance companies adjust their portfolios more slowly, as they are investing in assets with longer maturity. However, loans from insurance companies are not sensitive to GHG emission intensity. The implication is that insurance companies avoid high emitters, even if those firms are efficient in terms of emissions intensity.

Nevertheless, to uncover the specific mechanisms of the emissions effect on insurance company lending, we need more detailed information on insurance company decision-making processes regarding loan provisions. Unfortunately, such information is currently unavailable. Therefore, further investigation of this will be a topic for future research.

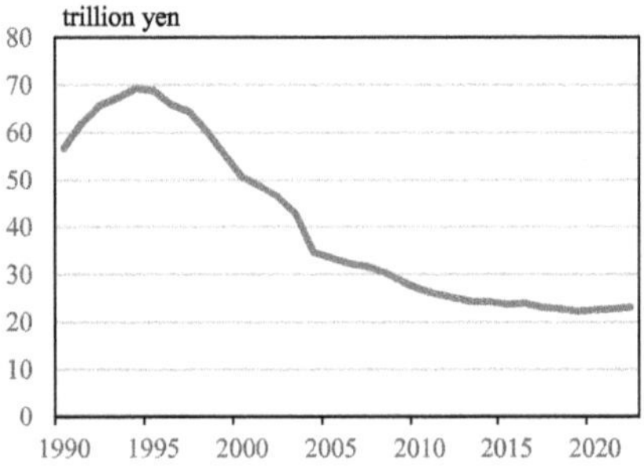

Fig. 4 Loans by insurance companies. *Source* Bank of Japan

Table 11 Effect of GHG emissions on loans by insurance companies

	(1) Δ LOAN	(2) Δ LOAN
GHGL1	−0.877* (0.469)	
GHGI1		−0.444 (0.709)
Finn ROA	−0.0580 (0.114)	−0.0657 (0.0999)
Firm ROA	0.802** (0.323)	0.332 (0.255)
Firm size	−0.517 (1.697)	−1.005 (1.683)
N	5833	4856
R^2	0.013	0.013
Year fixed effect	Yes	Yes
Insurance company fixed effect	Yes	Yes

Note * $p < 0.10$, ** $p < 0.05$, *** $p < 0.01$. Clustered standard errors at the year and insurance company levels are shown in parentheses. The table shows the results of the panel regressions, where the dependent variable is insurance companies' loan growth rate to listed firms

4 Conclusion

In this chapter, we investigate the effect of GHG emissions on bank loans using bank–firm loan data for Japanese listed firms from 2006 to 2022. We find that loans to high GHG emitters, in terms of level and intensity, are associated with lower loan growth rates. The effect is economically significant; the 25 and 75 percentiles of the contribution of the GHG emission level on loans are -1.66 and 1.35 percentage points, respectively. In addition, we provide evidence that the effect of GHG emissions is driven mainly by supply-side rather than demand-side factors. Furthermore, we provide evidence that insurance company loans are also affected by borrowers' GHG emission levels.

However, some limitations to our study warrant comment. First, the data on GHG emissions include estimates provided by the evaluation company Trucost. Previous studies point out that estimation models may not accurately capture true emission levels. This suggests that the association between GHG emissions and loans may arise from the model or variables used to estimate GHG emissions. Notably, the strong relationship between GHG emissions and bank loans has economic implications, even if they are merely estimates of GHG emissions. This is because the GHG emission estimation is considered among the best based on available information. Therefore, if banks allocate fewer loans to firms labeled as high emitters based on external information, this practice could contribute to a more energy-efficient and greener economy.

Second, the GHG emission variables could proxy firms' attitudes toward climate issues and environmental concerns. This may encompass, for example, their investment stance in new and efficient machinery. In this chapter, we do not mean to imply that banks should only consider GHG emission variables as evaluation measures of firms' greenness. We rather believe that GHG emission variables serve as useful proxies for banks to evaluate borrowing firms.

Third, we focus solely on the Scope 1 GHG emissions and do not delve into Scope 2 and 3 variables. As regulations governing direct emissions (i.e., Scope 1) become increasingly stringent, firms may resort to using affiliated entities to mask and outsource their GHG emissions. The literature has uncovered evidence of this "regulatory arbitrage" (See for example, Bartram et al. 2022). However, the measurement challenges associated with data for Scope 2 and Scope 3 are more pronounced than those for Scope 1. To obtain a comprehensive understanding of the relationship between GHG emissions and bank loans, going forward, we need to devise a method that incorporates these variables into our analysis. Furthermore, the correlations among the GHG emission variables in Scope 1, 2, and 3 are so high that it is difficult to econometrically isolate each effect.

In this chapter, we do not investigate the effect of credit allocation on firm activity, such as fixed asset investment. It is unclear whether an increase in bank loan provisions will lead to an increase in green investments by the borrowing firms. To reveal the nexus between allocation and its contribution to the green economy, further investigation is needed using more detailed data on firm environmental activity, as has been extensively discussed by international and domestic authorities. Additionally, in this chapter, we do not study loans to small- and medium-sized firms because data on GHG emissions and bank loans at the firm level are not easily accessible. However, the share of loans to small- and medium-sized firms constitutes approximately half of the Japanese bank loan market. Therefore, these loans should be considered to obtain a more comprehensive view of the relationship between loans and borrowers' GHG emissions. Finally, the importance of non-bank financial institutions as credit instrument providers has been increasing, especially after the global financial crisis. Therefore, it is essential to understand their investment behavior and incentivize them to increase investment in greener firms to create a greener economy.

References

Aruga, R., K., Chiba, T., and Goshima, K. (2022): "CO2 Emissions and corporate performance: Japan's evidence with double machine learning," Institute for Monetary and Economic Studies, Bank of Japan, Discussion paper series 2022-E-1.

Aswani, J., Raghunandan, A., and Rajgopal, S. (2023): "Are carbon emissions associated with stock returns?" Review of Finance, forthcoming.

Bartram, S. M., Hou, K., and Kim, S. (2022): "Real effects of climate policy: Financial constraints and spillovers." Journal of Financial Economics, 143(2), 668–696.

Becker, B. and Ivashina, V. (2014): "Cyclicality of credit supply: Firm level evidence," Journal of Monetary Economics, 62, 76–93. 28.

Benincasa, E. Kabas, G. and Ongena, S. (2022): "'There is No Planet B. There are Countries B to Z': Domestic Climate Policy and Cross-Border Lending." Swiss Finance Institute Research Paper, 22–28.

Bolton, P. and Kacperczyk, M. (2021): "Do investors care about carbon risk?" Journal of Financial Economics, 142, 517–549.

Chava, S. (2014): "Environmental externalities and cost of capital," Management science, 60, 2223–2247.

Ehlers, T., F. Packer, and de Greiff, K. (2022): "The pricing of carbon risk in syndicated loans: which risks are priced and why?" Journal of Banking & Finance, 136, 106180.

Flammer, C. (2021): "Corporate green bonds," Journal of Financial Economics, 142(2), 499–516.

Fujii, H., Iwata, K., Kaneko, S., and Managi, S. (2013): "Corporate environmental and economic performance of Japanese manufacturing firms: Empirical study for sustainable development," Business Strategy and the Environment, 22, 187–201.

Garvey, G., Iyer, M., and Nash J. (2018): "Carbon footprint and productivity: does the 'E' in ESG capture efficiency as well as environment?" Journal of Investment Management, 16, 59–69.

Ge, W. and Liu, M. (2015): "Corporate social responsibility and the cost of corporate bonds." Journal of Accounting and Public Policy, 34(6), 597–624.

Goss, A. and Roberts, G. S. (2011): "The impact of corporate social responsibility on the cost of bank loans," Journal of Banking & Finance, 35, 1794–1810.

Hasan, I., Hoi, C. K., Wu, Q., and Zhang, H. (2017): "Social capital and debt contracting: Evidence from bank loans and public bonds," Journal of Financial and Quantitative Analysis, 52, 1017–1047.

Hauptmann, C. (2017): "Corporate sustainability performance and bank loan pricing: It pays to be good, but only when banks are too," Said Business School WP, 20.

Hoshi, T. and Kashyap, A. (1999): "The Japanese Banking Crisis: Where did it come from and how will it end?" NBER Macroeconomics Annual, 14, 129–201.

Houston, J. F. and Shan, H. (2022): "Corporate ESG profiles and banking relationships," The Review of Financial Studies, 35, 3373–3417.

In, S. Y., Park, K. Y., and Monk, A. (2017): "Is 'being green' rewarded in the market?: An empirical investigation of decarbonization risk and stock returns," International Association for Energy Economics (Singapore Issue), 46(48).

International Monetary Fund (2023): Global Financial Stability Report, April 2023.

Kacperczyk, M. T. and Peydro, J.-L. (2021): "Carbon emissions and the bank-lending channel," CEPR Discussion Paper No. DP16778.

Kleimeier, S. and Viehs, M. (2018): "Carbon disclosure, emission levels, and the cost of debt," Emission Levels, and the Cost of Debt (January 7, 2018). 29.

Nishitani, K. and Kokubu, K. (2012): "Why does the reduction of greenhouse gas emissions enhance firm value? The case of Japanese manufacturing firms," Business Strategy and the Environment, 21, 517–529.

Okimoto, T. and Takaoka, S. (2021): "Sustainability and Credit Spreads in Japan," Research Institute of Economy, Trade and Industry (RIETI).

Ongena, S., M. Delis, and K. de Greiff (2018): "Being stranded on the carbon bubble? Climate policy risk and the pricing of bank loans," CEPR Discussion Paper No. DP12928.

Reghezza, A., Altunbas, Y., Marques-Ibanez, D., d'Acri, C. R., and Spaggiari, M. (2022): "Do banks fuel climate change?" Journal of Financial Stability, 62, 101049.

Scatigna, M., Xia, D., Zabai, A., and Zulaica, O. (2021): "Achievements and challenges in ESG markets," BIS Quarterly Review, December.

Sharfman, M. P. and Fernando, C. S. (2008): "Environmental risk management and the cost of capital," Strategic Management Journal, 29, 569–592.

Shirasu, Y., and Kawakita, H. (2021): "Long-term financial performance of corporate social responsibility," Global Finance Journal, 50, 100532.

Takahashi, K. and Shino, J. (2023): “Greenhouse gas emissions and bank lending,” BIS Working Paper, 1078.
Trucost (2018): “Trucost environmental register: Methodology FAQs.”
Zerbib, O. D. (2019): “The effect of pro-environmental preferences on bond prices: Evidence from green bonds,” Journal of Banking and Finance, 98, 39–60.

Environmental Innovation and CO_2 Emissions in Asian Countries

Somin Lee and Doo Bong Han

1 Introduction

The world's tremendous economic growth has been accompanied by largely unsustainable development, which has led to a considerable increase in the emission of pollutants. As a result, many environmental issues, like pollution and climate change due to the rapid global population increase, have arisen affecting energy demand, urbanization, and industrialization (Choi and Han 2018). Environmental problems pose the greatest threat to both human civilization and ecosystems, as they impact almost every aspect of human life, including food, health, trade, and transportation infrastructure (Cramer et al. 2018). Therefore, it is important that we gain a better understanding of the relationship between economic performance and environmental sustainability, as humanity faces the difficult challenge of climate change.

An important global environmental issue is the severity of global warming. Human economic activities, such as deforestation and tourism, generate greenhouse gases (GHG), which are primarily responsible for global warming, accounting for more than 95% of these (Mongo et al. 2021; Atasoy 2017). Since 75% of the world's greenhouse gas emissions come from carbon dioxide (CO_2), several previous studies have used carbon emissions as a measure of environmental pollution (Tiba and Omri 2017). Consequently, many countries have been actively pursuing the common climate goals established in the Paris Agreement in 2016 and at the UN Climate Action Summit in 2019 to reduce carbon dioxide emissions and are beginning to discuss the global agenda of "net-zero emissions by 2050" as a specific outcome.

S. Lee
Department of Food and Resource Economics, Korea University, 145 Anam-Ro, Seongbuk-Gu, Seoul 02841, Korea

D. B. Han (✉)
Department of Food and Resource Economics, Korea University and President, Korea Rural Economic Institute, 601 Bitgaram-Ro, Naju-Si, Jeollanamdo 58321, Korea
e-mail: dbhan@krei.re.kr

S. Takaoka (ed.), *Environmental Technology Innovation and ESG Investment*,
https://doi.org/10.1007/978-981-99-9768-8_5

Asia is the largest emitter of GHG worldwide and the predominant source of the global CO_2 emissions, accounting for 53% of the total with its coal consumption exceeding 60%. China is the foremost offender, discharging almost 10 billion tons of CO_2 each year, representing over one-fourth of the total global emissions, establishing itself as the world's principal CO_2 emitter (Global Carbon Project, 2017). Furthermore, other Asian countries, such as India, Japan, and South Korea, are also prominent CO_2 emitters (OECD Data: Air and GHG emissions). However, many Asian countries are also classified as developing economies. Thus, environmental protection is not the main focus of economic policies in Asia because these countries are still in the initial phases of economic development. Additionally, their high reliance on fossil fuels and lack of renewable energy technology contribute to high CO_2 emissions. These factors increase the need to reduce CO_2 emissions in Asian countries to ensure environmental sustainability.

As the importance of reducing carbon emissions continues to be emphasized, environmental innovation has become a practical solution for achieving environmental sustainability and, consequently, a priority for governments worldwide (Ahmad et al. 2020; Töbelmann and Wendler 2020). Environmental innovation can enhance energy efficiency and minimize pollution (Du et al. 2019; Fernández et al. 2018). It encompasses the development of environmentally friendly products and technologies, and systems that can promote environmentally friendly production. Notably, environmental innovation plays an important role in the relationship between economic growth and environmental improvement. Therefore, environmental innovation needs to be emphasized to solve current environmental problems and ensure future environmental sustainability, particularly in Asia.

The objective of this study is to identify the relationship between environmental innovation and CO_2 emissions in 26 Asian countries. We divide Asian countries into high- and middle-income and high- and low-government effectiveness. This categorization allows us to explore the differences and patterns in the ways in which environmental innovation affects CO_2 emissions. Many studies have emphasized environmental innovation as an effective approach for achieving both economic development and environmental sustainability. Studies have demonstrated that environmental innovation can improve environmental quality (Ahmad et al. 2022; Du et al. 2019). However, empirical evidence regarding the claim that environmental innovations have positive effects on climate change is limited (Su and Moaniba 2017). In fact, some studies argue that environmental innovation either worsens environmental quality or has no impact on it (Dauda et al. 2021). Studies analyzing this relationship in Asian countries are lacking. Our investigation is unique as we focus exclusively on the relationship between environmental innovation and CO_2 emissions in Asian countries. We expect that our results can provide policymakers, scholars, and organizations with reference data to address climate change and promote sustainable development.

2 Literature Review

An increasing number of studies have investigated the link between environmental innovation and CO_2 emissions using environment-related public and private research and development (R&D) and environmental technology patents as measures of environmental innovation (Du et al. 2019; Fernández et al. 2018). Such studies have been particularly frequent in the Organization for Economic Co-operation and Development (OECD) countries and there have also been several studies in developing countries and domestic regions (Fatima et al. 2023; Hashmi and Alam 2019; Pata et al. 2023; Tan and Cao 2023; Yıldırım et al. 2022). Studies show that the impact of environmental innovation on environmental quality varies across countries.

The previous studies have shown that environmental innovation reduces CO_2 emissions. For example, Choi and Han (2018) examine the effects of environmental innovation, gross domestic product (GDP), trade, foreign direct investment (FDI), and other factors on CO_2 and sulphur dioxide (SO_2) emissions in high- and middle-income countries. Their results show that only in high-income countries environmental innovation leads to a decrease in both SO_2 and CO_2 emissions over time, but with no significant impact in middle-income countries. Additionally, the Environmental Kuznets Curve (EKC) is reflected only in high-income countries. Similar to Choi and Han (2018), Milindi and Inglesi-Lotz (2022) analyze different income groups and the relationship between environmental innovation and CO_2 emissions. Looking at 1989 to 2018, after dividing 45 countries into high-, upper-middle-, and lower-middle-income groups, they investigate the impact of green technology and renewable energy on CO_2 emissions. They also use environmental patents as the indicator of environmental technology. Their results demonstrate that green innovation only reduce CO_2 emissions in countries with very high income levels, whereas renewable energy decreases CO_2 emissions in all groups. Du et al. (2019), focusing on 71 countries, analyzes the impact of environment-related technology on CO_2 emissions using the panel threshold model. Specifically, the authors investigate whether income levels influence the effectiveness of environmental innovation. The results show that in countries where income levels exceed a certain threshold, green innovation has a mitigating effect on CO_2 emissions, whereas it does not significantly contribute to CO_2 emissions reduction in countries below that threshold. The authors conclude that while green technological innovation is only effective when an economy reaches a high-income level, it does play an important role in climate change mitigation. Töbelmann and Wendler (2020) analyze the impact of environmental innovation on CO_2 emissions by focusing on 27 European Union (EU) countries. They use number of patent applications related to the environment as the indicator of environmental innovation and find that such patents play a role in mitigating CO_2 emissions. However, their effect is insufficient to offset the increase in CO_2 emissions caused by economic growth. Using data from 18 emerging countries, Ahmad et al. (2022) show how environmental innovation, economic globalization, energy productivity, and GDP influence the ecological footprint. Their results reveal that environmental innovation and energy productivity contribute to reducing the ecological footprint, while economic globalization increases the ecological footprint and deteriorates environmental quality. Hashmi and Alam (2019) investigate the correlation between key elements affecting CO_2 emissions in OECD countries. Their analysis reveals that a 1% increase in green patents results in a 0.017% decrease in CO_2 emissions, while a 1% increase in per capita environmental taxes leads to a 0.03% decrease.

The number of studies of Asian countries has also increased since 1995. Naz and Aslam (2023) estimate the relationship between environmental innovation, financial improvement, globalization, governance, and CO_2 emissions in South Asian countries. According to their results, environmental innovation reduces carbon emissions, whereas financial development, globalization, and governance contribute to increasing CO_2 emissions. Mohd Suki et al. (2022) analyze how environment-related technology innovation affects CO_2 emissions in six ASEAN countries–Malaysia, Singapore, the Philippines, Indonesia, Thailand, and Vietnam–from 1992 to 2018. The findings show that renewable energy consumption and green technology innovation decrease CO_2 emissions, whereas the consumption of non-renewable energy increases them. Saleem et al. (2022) analyze the impact of income, environmental taxes, green growth, eco-friendly technology, and renewable energy on environmental quality in 12 Asian countries. Their results reveal an inverse causal relationship between CO_2 emissions and all variables except GDP growth. Wen et al. (2022) examine the effects of environmental innovation on CO_2 emissions in five South Asian countries. According to their results, environmental patents in South Asian countries significantly reduce CO_2 emissions.

However, other studies have shown that environmental innovation has no notable influence on CO_2 emissions reduction and may even lead to an increase. Danish and Ulucak (2020) analyze the influence of variables, such as environmental patents, GDP, and renewable energy, on CO_2 emissions in the US and China. Their results reveal that technological innovation in the US decreases CO_2 emissions, whereas these results are not observed in China. In contrast to the other Asian studies mentioned earlier, Mehmood (2023) demonstrates that technological innovation, trade, and economic growth act as factors that worsen the environment. According to Yıldırım et al. (2022), environmental innovations do not always reduce CO_2 emissions. Specifically, the authors investigate the nonlinear relationship between environmental innovation and environmental quality across 32 OECD countries. According to their study, environmental innovation has no impact on reducing CO_2 emissions below a certain threshold (1st regime). However, once this threshold is reached, a reduction effect becomes apparent (2nd regime). Beyond that threshold, environmental innovation results in an increase in CO_2 emissions (3rd regime). Therefore, the study suggests that environmental issues cannot be resolved solely through environmental innovation and emphasizes the need for support from environmental policies. Dauda et al. (2021) examine the nonlinear relationship between environmental innovation and CO_2 emissions in nine African countries. Their results reveal a reverse U-shaped curve between environmental innovation and CO_2 emissions in several African countries. Specifically, in the initial stages of environmental innovation, CO_2 emissions increase; however, higher levels of innovation lead to a decrease. Focusing on the countries Brazil, Russia, India, China, and South Africa

(BRICS), Cheng et al. (2019) analyze the effects of several factors, including environmental innovation, renewable energy, FDI, GDP, and exports, on CO_2 emissions reduction using panel data spanning approximately 15 years. The results indicate that renewable energy and FDI contribute to a decrease in CO_2 emissions, while environmental innovation does not in these countries. In fact, they show a trend of even higher CO_2 emission levels. Tan and Cao (2023) analyze the link between green innovation and CO_2 emissions in G7 and BRICS countries. In their study, both CO_2 emissions and CO_2 intensity are used as indicators of emissions, while four indicators are used for green technology. The findings indicate that single-type green technology innovation either has no impact on CO_2 emissions or mostly leads to an increase. However, the interaction between these types of green technology innovation has an influence on CO_2 reduction. Dauda et al. (2019) reveal that innovation reduces CO_2 emissions in G6 countries, representing advanced economies. However, it leads to an increase in emissions in MENA countries (Egypt, Bahrain, Morocco, Algeria, Tunisia, the United Arab Emirates, and Israel) and the BRICS countries. As a result, the authors suggest that G6 countries should facilitate innovation in developing countries, and nations should make efforts to integrate advanced technologies related to CO_2 emissions reduction potential through FDI.

Based on a comprehensive review of previous studies, we can see that the relationship between environmental innovation and CO_2 emissions varies. Additionally, some studies have conducted their analyses at a national level. While others have investigated how environmental innovation affects CO_2 emissions in specific Asian regions, such as South or Southeast Asia. However, there is a lack of studies investigating a comprehensive range of Asian countries. Therefore, our objective is to analyze the relationship between environmental innovation and CO_2 emissions across all Asian countries. A distinctive feature of this study is that we consider different patterns of environmental innovation and CO_2 emissions based on income and government effectiveness.

3 Data and Methodology

3.1 Theoretical Framework

This study is based on a theoretical exploration of the relationships among CO_2 emissions and environmental innovation, trade, FDI, GDP, urbanization, renewable energy, and manufacturing. Environmental innovation has been shown to play a crucial role in reducing CO_2 emissions and the impact of climate change. Researchers have defined environmental innovation in various ways. Environmental innovation refers to "new combinations of production factors chosen to produce processes, products or service that create less burden on the environment" or "new measures that companies select to cope with environmental problems." This can include not only the development of environmentally friendly technologies, but also eco-friendly products and materials, the introduction of systems that promote environmentally friendly production, and the adoption of policies that promote environmental sustainability. Thus, environmental innovation encompasses activities that involve creating or improving production processes, technologies, or systems to reduce or eliminate the negative environmental impacts of destructive human activities (Naz and Aslam 2023). Environmental innovation also refers to the acceptability of innovative ideas that focus on sustainability (Wijethilake et al. 2018).

However, while such broad definitions of environmental innovation can explain various phenomena, they pose difficulties in analysis. Therefore, many studies use patents and R&D in environment-related technologies as indicators of environmental innovation. Patents are favored because they include comprehensive information about each innovation and tend to represent the commercial market output better than R&D does (OECD). Therefore, based on several previous studies, we adopt environmental patents as a proxy for environmental innovation. We include environmental patents with one-year to two-year lagged environmental patents to account for time-delayed feedback, as environmental patents can have an impact on CO_2 emissions with time delays (Choi and Han 2018).

As a measure of income, GDP per capita can be used. Increased economic activity can increase production and consumption, resulting in higher CO_2 emissions. In other words, GDP indirectly influences CO_2 emissions through various factors, such as changes in land use, consumer behavior, and industrial structures, rather than causing them to increase directly. However, the square of GDP presents a nonlinear relationship between the environment and income, indicating a negative relationship between higher income levels and lower CO_2 emissions. This relationship is commonly referred to as the Environmental Kuznets Curve (EKC), which provides a graphical representation of an inverted U-shape. According to the EKC, environmental degradation occurs in the initial phases of economic development, while environmental improvement occurs once economic growth reaches a particular level. This transition can be attributed to several factors, such as investments in low-carbon and renewable energy technologies, increased awareness of the environment by society, and changes in consumer behavior (Naz and Aslam 2023). In fact, many previous studies have investigated this relationship and their findings suggest that economic growth is directly linked to high production levels of goods and services, which leads to environmental degradation.

According to an IEA report (2018), a significant share of global CO_2 emissions originates from pollution associated with global trade. Consequently, many studies have investigated the correlation between CO_2 emissions and trade (Dauda et al. 2021; Handoyo et al. 2022; Sebri and Ben-Salha 2014). However, these studies have produced varying results, with no specific consensus reached. In other words, trade openness can have both a positive and negative impact on CO_2 emissions, influenced by two main mechanisms: scale effects and technological effects. First, scale effects assume that as trade increases, industrial activity and transportation also increase, promoting economic growth but resulting in increased CO_2 emissions, thus negatively affecting the environment (Adams and Acheampong 2019; Usman et al. 2020). However, owing to technological effects, trade openness motivates countries to adopt cleaner technologies. Some also argue that when benefiting from knowledge transfer through environmentally friendly trade, countries can reduce emissions (Ike et al. 2020).

The effect of FDI on CO_2 emissions can also be positive or negative. On the one hand, in improving the economy, FDI can increase pollution. In other words, FDI can lead to environmental degradation by increasing industrial activities. Additionally, FDI has typically depended on the production of minerals and the use of natural resources, such as gas and oil. Countries with less strict environmental regulations are more likely to attract resources and pollution-intensive industries. Therefore, environmental degradation is predicted to result from FDI inflows into host countries lacking sufficient regulatory measures for environmental protection. According to To et al. (2019), FDI in Asian countries has a linear relationship with environmental degradation. On the other hand, other studies suggest that foreign companies introducing more eco-friendly technologies can have a positive effect on domestic companies by promoting more efficient resource utilization and reducing CO_2 emissions (Gormus and Aydin 2020; Mert and Caglar 2020).

Urbanization refers to the social phenomenon in which people move from rural areas to cities to find an environment that is more suited to their needs. Previous research has examined the connection between urbanization and CO_2 emissions with varying conclusions. As Du et al. (2012) argue, the relationship between the degree of urbanization and CO_2 emissions can be uncertain. First, urbanization inevitably promotes the development of urban infrastructure, which can stimulate energy consumption and increase CO_2 emissions. Conversely, as the focal point of regional development, urban areas have strong agglomeration effects and can thus reduce CO_2 emissions through the scale effect of energy usage. Furthermore, studies by Lin et al. (2017) and Zhang et al. (2017) have shown the existence of an inverse U-shaped relationship between CO_2 emissions and urbanization. They indicate that during the initial stages of urbanization, emissions may increase, but once urbanization reaches a certain level, emissions can decrease.

Renewable energy refers to the production of energy from infinite resources or resources that use considerably less CO_2 compared with fossil fuels, like coal and oil. Therefore, the expansion of renewable energy use is increasingly important in many countries, as it can simultaneously address issues of fossil fuel depletion and the need for environmental improvement. Our study includes the impact of renewable energy consumption on CO_2 emissions based on these previous studies (Du et al. 2019; Milindi and Inglesi-Lotz 2022; Mohd Suki et al. 2022; Töbelmann and Wendler 2020). We also consider the manufacturing sector, which reflects industrial structure, as a variable that contributes to a country's energy usage and CO_2 emissions directly associated with economic growth, showcasing the industrial characteristics of a nation.

3.2 Data

We use panel data from the World Bank and the OECD covering 1990–2019 to investigate the effects of environmental innovation on CO_2 emissions. First, considering that the long-run association between CO_2 emissions and the explanatory variables can vary, depending on the stage of development (Choi and Han 2018; Milindi and Inglesi-Lotz 2022; Nasrullah et al. 2023; Sharma 2011), we classify the countries into income groups based on the 2019 World Bank income classification (Table 1).

The impact of green innovation on CO_2 emissions can differ depending on various conditions, such as income level and time, leading to the potential for both an increase and decrease in emissions (Milindi and Inglesi-Lotz 2022). High-income countries have greater financial resources and technological capabilities, making it easier for them to adopt and implement environmental innovation. In contrast, low-income countries may lack the necessary infrastructure to support the implementation of environmental innovation due to economic constraints. Furthermore, in developing countries, the absence of cooperative policies and environmental regulations for technology transfer from advanced countries creates uncertainty regarding the impact of green technology on CO_2 emissions. The lack of environmental regulations can impede the spread of environmental technology, leading to less effect on CO_2 emissions (Cheng et al. 2019). Therefore, our aim is to analyze the relationship between environmental innovation and CO_2 emissions, dividing Asian countries into high- and middle-income countries, and considering the potential differences between them based on variations in financial capabilities.

Furthermore, government effectiveness is essential for the success of environmental policies as well as for environmental innovation (Gani and Scrimgeour 2014; Khan and Rana 2021; Nair et al. 2021). In other words, essential elements that can help reduce environmental degradation include government resilience against political pressure, the effectiveness of policy formulation and implementation, and the reliability of government dedication to these policies (Al-Mulali et al. 2022; World Bank 2021). Thus, we also classify countries in terms of high and low government effectiveness based on the government effectiveness index in the World Bank's World Development Indicators (Table 2).

Table 1 Country classification by income level

High income (10)	Middle income (16)	
	Upper middle (11)	Lower middle (5)
Australia, Cyprus, Israel, Japan, Korea, Kuwait, New Zealand, Saudi Arabia, Singapore, United Arab Emirates	Armenia, China, Georgia, Indonesia, Iran, Jordan, Kazakhstan, Lebanon, Malaysia, Thailand, Turkey	India, Sri Lanka, Pakistan, Philippines, Uzbekistan

Note World Bank Classification (GNI per capita in US$, 2015); High Income (>$12,535), Upper-Middle Income ($4,046 ~ 12,535), Lower-Middle Income ($1,036 ~ 4,045), Lower Income (≤$1,025)

Table 2 Country classification by government effectiveness

High effectiveness (10)	Low effectiveness (16)
Australia, Cyprus, Georgia, Israel, Japan, Korea, Malaysia, New Zealand, Singapore, United Arab Emirates	Armenia, China, India, Indonesia, Iran, Jordan, Kazakhstan, Kuwait, Lebanon, Pakistan, Philippines, Saudi Arabia, Sri Lanka, Thailand, Turkey, Uzbekistan

Note (1) The source of government effectiveness index is the World Development Indicators (WDI), 2019; (2) The index scale ranges from a negative value of −2.5, representing very low, to a positive value of +2.5, indicating very high; (3) K-means clustering analysis is used to divide countries into two groups

Countries with high government effectiveness scores have politically independent governments, with a greater focus on policy implementation and higher-quality policy formulation. In contrast, countries with low government effectiveness face challenges, such as weak institutional capacity and inefficient policy implementation. Therefore, countries with higher government effectiveness are expected to more likely mitigate pollution than countries with lower government effectiveness are (Al-Mulali et al. 2022). As the World Bank does not provide rankings based on its government effectiveness index, we use k-means clustering to classify countries into these two groups.

The data sources in this study are as follows: The data for environmental innovation come from the OECD, while the data for government effective come from the World Bank Development Indicators (WDI) database. Table 3 presents the sources, measurements, and definitions of the variables. Table 4 provides summary statistics of the full sample data we use in the analysis.

Table 5 presents the basic statistics for the subsample. Considering the division based on government effectiveness, when examining the dependent variable $\ln CO_2$, the average in the high-effectiveness group is 2.1074, whereas, it is 1.0851 in the low-effectiveness group. Thus, the average $\ln CO_2$ is higher in countries with

Table 3 Data source and description of variables

Variable	Description	Unit	Source
CO_2	Carbon emissions	Metric tons per capita	WDI
EI	Patents for environmental technologies	Count	OECD
GDP	GDP per capita	Constant 2015 US$	WDI
TRADE	Trade	% of GDP	WDI
FDI	FDI net inflow	% of GDP	WDI
URBAN	Urban population	% of total population	WDI
REC	Renewable energy consumption	% of total final energy consumption	WDI
MANU	Manufacturing value added	% of GDP	WDI

Table 4 Data description of variables in the full sample

Variable	Mean	Std. Dev	Min	Max
lnCO_2	1.4783	1.0709	−1.5069	3.4427
lnEI	2.4775	2.5553	−2.4853	8.9490
t-1	2.4363	2.5429	−2.4853	8.9490
t-2	2.4119	2.5217	−2.4853	8.9490
lnGDP	8.9047	1.2838	6.2708	11.0759
$(\text{lnGDP})^2$	80.9392	22.9265	39.3229	122.6746
lnTRADE	4.2399	0.6049	2.7412	6.0807
lnFDI	0.5328	1.5826	−7.9014	5.6325
lnURBAN	4.1045	0.4230	2.9012	4.6052
lnREC	1.5954	2.1010	−4.7069	4.3578
lnMANU	2.6983	0.4507	1.3571	3.4798

Table 5 Data description of variables of the subsamples

Group	Variable	Mean	Std. dev	Min	Max
High income	lnCO_2	2.4463	0.4665	1.7062	3.4427
	lnEI	3.6359	2.5039	−1.9456	8.9490
Middle income	lnCO_2	0.8733	0.8807	−1.5069	2.7370
	lnEI	1.5279	2.1807	−2.4853	8.5090
High effectiveness	lnCO_2	2.1074	0.6956	−0.2963	3.4302
	lnEI	3.4315	2.5696	−1.9456	8.9490
Low effectiveness	lnCO_2	1.0851	1.0772	−1.5069	3.4427
	lnEI	1.6182	2.2186	−2.4853	8.5090

high government effectiveness. Similarly, for the key independent variable lnEI, it is evident that environmental innovation is higher in high-effectiveness countries than in low-effectiveness countries. Generally, high-income countries have high government effectiveness as well; thus, the basic statistics of high-income and high government effectiveness are similar. However, high-income countries have both higher levels of CO_2 emissions and environmental innovation. Furthermore, when comparing middle-income countries with low government effectiveness ones, we see that the averages for CO_2 emissions and environmental innovation in the group with low government effectiveness are slightly higher than those in the middle-income group.

3.3 Methodology

We apply a panel analysis to investigate the impact of environmental innovation on CO_2 emissions. Our main objective is to assess the direct influence of environmental innovation on CO_2 emissions by evaluating the results of innovation rather than the inputs to innovation.

This study applies a logarithmic transformation to all variables to ensure variance stability. The empirical model is as follows:

$$\begin{aligned} lnCO2_{it} = {} & \beta_1 lnEI_{it-j} + \beta_2 lnGDP_{it} + \beta_3 ln(GDP)^2_{it} + \beta_4 lnTRADE_{it} \\ & + \beta_5 FDI_{it} + \beta_6 lnURBAN_{it} + \beta_7 lnREC_{it} \\ & + \beta_8 lnMANU_{it} + \mu_i + \upsilon_t + e_{it} \end{aligned} \quad (1)$$

In the Eq. (1), i represents the country and t the year. The dependent variable CO_2 represents the CO_2 emissions per capita in country i. The independent variable EI is the crucial focus of this research, as it measures environmental innovation activity through environmental patent applications. We use this to examine the relationship between environmental innovation and CO_2 emissions reduction. The lagged variable of EI accounts for the time interval, as environmental innovation may take time to affect CO_2 emissions. GDP represents GDP per capita and $(GDP)^2$ represents the squared term of GDP per capita. To account for the nonlinear relationship between income and CO_2 emissions, the model includes a squared term of GDP. We also investigate how income affects CO_2 emissions over time. In other words, we aim to verify the EKC hypothesis that income initially causes environmental pollution during economic growth, but eventually helps to improve the environment after reaching a certain level. $TRADE$ represents the international trade proportion of GDP, indicating the degree of economic openness; and FDI is foreign direct investment inflow (% of GDP). $URBAN$ represents the share of the urban population to the total population, and the REC variable indicates the proportion of renewable energy consumption to total energy consumption. $MANU$ represents the manufacturing proportion of GDP. μ_i denotes the unobservable country-specific effect, υ_t represents the time effect, and e_{it} represents the idiosyncratic error term that varies depending on country and time.

Here, we use a panel analysis to investigate the impact of environmental innovation on environmental improvement, particularly CO_2 emissions reduction. For panel data, which are both cross-sectional and a time-series, the assumption of homoscedasticity of the error term may be violated or there may be a high probability of autocorrelation. Therefore, estimating panel data through a pooled OLS regression can result in omitted variable bias because of the difficulty in considering the heterogeneity of unobserved entities, which can lead to inconsistent estimates. As we analyze the impact of environmental innovation on CO_2 emissions with the Asian panel data, one problem is bias due to unobservable country-specific characteristics. If environmental innovation is correlated with these characteristics, the OLS method produces biased estimates. To solve this problem, we need to use a panel data analysis method that considers individual panel characteristics in the error term.

The commonly used panel data models are one-way and two-way error component models. These two models are expressed in Eqs. (2) and (3), respectively.

$$y_{it} = \alpha + \beta x_{it} + \mu_i + e_{it} \tag{2}$$

$$y_{it} = \alpha + \beta x_{it} + \mu_i + \upsilon_t + e_{it} \tag{3}$$

where, y_{it} and x_{it} represent the dependent variable and explanatory variable, respectively, and β represents the coefficients. μ_i is assumed to be the unobserved group heterogeneity error term, and υ_t is assumed to be the unobserved time heterogeneity error term that affects all groups in common. e_{it} is a pure error term that varies depending on both the group and time. Therefore, the Eq. (2) which specifies the error term as the factor that varies only for the group (μ_i) in addition to the factor that varies depending on the group and time (e_{it}), is called the one-way error component model. Equation (3), which includes the error term as the factor that varies depending on the group and time (e_{it}), the factor that varies only for the group (μ_i), and the factor that varies only for the time (υ_t), is called the two-way error component model.

These models are divided into the fixed effects and random effects models based on how the group-specific error term μ_i and the time-specific error term υ_t are considered. In general, if these error terms are assumed to be fixed and regarded as the parameters to be estimated, a fixed-effects model is applied. If the individual panel sample is a random sample drawn from the population, the error term is considered a random variable, and a random-effects model is applied. The fixed-effects model has the advantage of providing robust coefficient estimates even in the presence of endogenous explanatory variables. However, it is less efficient than the random-effects model when all explanatory variables are exogenous. This study uses the Hausman test to determine the appropriate model between fixed effect model and random effects model.

4 Results

4.1 Full Sample Results

The results for entire sample, as shown in Table 6, demonstrate that environmental innovation reduces CO_2 emissions in all columns, including the one-year and two-year lagged variables. The coefficient on environmental innovation is −0.02 to −0.01, which means that a 1% increase in environmental innovation decreases CO_2 emissions by 0.01% to 0.02%. Furthermore, the GDP coefficient is positive and statistically significant, while GDP squared is negative and statistically significant. This confirms that, in the overall sample, environmental improvement and economic

Table 6 Full sample results

Variables	CO_2 per capita		
	Full sample		
	(1)	(2)	(3)
$lnEI_t$	−0.0175[a] (0.0058)		
$lnEI_{t-1}$		−0.0234[a] (0.0058)	
$lnEI_{t-2}$			−0.0220[a] (0.0055)
lnGDPt	2.2037[a] (0.1607)	2.3163[a] (0.1660)	2.3703[a] (0.1654)
$(lnGDP)^2t$	−0.0922[a] (0.0091)	−0.0975[a] (0.0094)	−0.0989[a] (0.0094)
lnTRADE	0.0141 (0.0319)	0.0280 (0.0323)	0.0177 (0.0309)
$lnFDI_t$	0.0008 (0.0059)	0.0014 (0.0061)	0.0008 (0.0057)
$lnURBAN_t$	0.2631[b] (0.1125)	0.2547[b] (0.1165)	0.1810 (0.1171)
$lnREC_t$	−0.0816[a] (0.0182)	−0.0695[a] (0.0179)	−0.0659[a] (0.0172)
$lnMANU_t$	0.2844[a] (0.0450)	0.2826[a] (0.0453)	0.2822[a] (0.0447)
R-squared	0.7781	0.7714	0.7773
Hausman test	417.64[a]	403.84[a]	389.40[a]

Note (1) [a], [b], and [c] indicate significance at the 1%, 5%, and 10% levels, respectively. (2) The analysis includes year dummies, but the results are not included here for brevity

growth are inversely correlated, supporting the EKC hypothesis. Regarding the other dependent variables, the coefficients on urbanization and manufacturing are positive, indicating an increase in carbon emissions, whereas the coefficient on renewable energy consumption is significantly negative, indicating a reduction in CO_2 emissions. Finally, trade openness and FDI do not significantly affect CO_2 emissions.

4.2 *Subsample Results*

Tables 7 and 8 present the subsample results of the effects of environmental innovation on CO_2 emissions. Table 7 classifies Asian countries by income level, with columns (1)–(3) representing high-income countries and columns (4)–(6) representing middle-income countries.

Table 7 Subsample results by income

Variables	CO_2 per capita					
	High income			Middle income		
	(1)	(2)	(3)	(4)	(5)	(6)
$lnEI_t$	−0.0393[a] (0.0105)			−0.0142[b] (0.0065)		
$lnEI_{t-1}$		−0.0478[a] (0.0101)			−0.0155[b] (0.0064)	
$lnEI_{t-2}$			−0.0406[a] (0.0103)			−0.0156[b] (0.0065)
$lnGDP_t$	5.0929[a] (0.8180)	4.7969[a] (0.8756)	4.7241[a] (0.9454)	0.7265[a] (0.2651)	0.826[a] (0.2751)	0.9222[a] (0.2927)
$(lnGDP)^2t$	−0.2337[a] (0.0400)	−0.2193[a] (0.0426)	−0.2141[a] (0.0456)	−0.0130 (0.0163)	−0.0189 (0.0169)	−0.0219 (0.0180)
lnTRADE	−0.0876 (0.0606)	−0.0968 (0.0591)	−0.1263[b] (0.0599)	0.1266[a] (0.0396)	0.1478[a] (0.0406)	0.1201[a] (0.0413)
$lnFDI_t$	−0.0073 (0.0064)	−0.0057 (0.0062)	−0.0022 (0.0061)	0.0215[b] (0.0087)	0.0240[b] (0.0096)	0.0189[b] (0.0093)
$lnURBAN_t$	0.9570[b]	0.9297[b]	1.1107[a]	0.0216	−0.0079	−0.1576
	(0.3696)	(0.3727)	(0.3583)	(0.1283)	(0.1348)	(0.1435)
$lnREC_t$	0.0170 (0.0211)	0.0288 (0.0210)	0.0237 (0.0207)	−0.2388[a] (0.0301)	−0.2404[a] (0.0289)	−0.2041[a] (0.0304)
$lnMANU_t$	0.3387[a] (0.0676)	0.3900[a] (0.0620)	0.3509[a] (0.0642)	0.0603 (0.0699)	−0.0260 (0.0707)	0.0676 (0.0750)
R-squared	0.6334	0.6272	0.6098	0.8892	0.8879	0.8797
Hausman Test	157.54[a]	156.83[a]	151.86[a]	206.75[a]	198.38[a]	188.79[a]

Note (1) [a], [b], and [c] indicate significance at the 1%, 5%, and 10% levels, respectively. (2) The analysis includes year dummies, but the results are not included for brevity

First, we can see that environmental innovation reduces CO_2 emissions in both high- and middle-income countries. As shown in columns (1)–(3), environmental innovation effectively mitigates CO_2 emissions in high-income countries. In other words, environmentally friendly production, technologies, and equipment reduce CO_2 emissions as these reduce the energy burden related to pollution in the production process, thus improving environmental quality (Dauda et al. 2021). Thus, encouraging environmentally friendly technologies and replacing traditional technologies with advanced ones can promote sustainable development.

Similarly, as shown in columns (4)–(6), environmental innovation also contributes to a decrease in CO_2 emissions in middle-income countries. However, looking at the coefficients for high-income countries, a 1% increase in environmental innovation leads to a 0.039–0.047% decrease in CO_2 emissions, whereas middle-income countries see only a 0.014–0.015% decrease. Comparing these findings with the results

Table 8 Subsample results by government effectiveness

Variables	CO_2 per capita					
	High effectiveness			Low effectiveness		
	(1)	(2)	(3)	(4)	(5)	(6)
$\ln EI_t$	−0.0152 (0.0099)			−0.0066 (0.0063)		
$\ln EI_{t-1}$		−0.0228[b] (0.0096)			−0.0066 (0.0063)	
$\ln EI_{t-2}$			−0.0277[a] (0.0094)			−0.0057 (0.0059)
$\ln GDP_t$	2.6258[a] (0.3599)	2.9533[a] (0.3543)	3.3368[a] (0.3515)	0.9823[a] (0.2391)	1.2034[a] (0.2507)	1.3403[a] (0.2455)
$(\ln GDP)^2 t$	−0.1004[a] (0.0199)	−0.1161[a] (0.0195)	−0.135[a] (0.0191)	−0.0309[b] (0.0147)	−0.0422[a] (0.0155)	−0.0462[a] (0.0153)
lnTRADE	0.0975[c] (0.0540)	0.1006[c] (0.0521)	0.0819 (0.0496)	0.0298 (0.0397)	0.0295 (0.0423)	0.0006 (0.0398)
$\ln FDI_t$	−0.0145[c] (0.0075)	−0.0194[a] (0.0071)	−0.0193[a] (0.0067)	0.0216[a] (0.0077)	0.0289[a] (0.0086)	0.0281[a] (0.0074)
$\ln URBAN_t$	1.5110[a] (0.2433)	1.5180[a] (0.2385)	1.4086[a] (0.2319)	−0.1256 (0.1128)	−0.1404 (0.1225)	−0.2473[b] (0.1226)
$\ln REC_t$	0.0112 (0.0219)	0.0295 (0.0214)	0.0283 (0.0202)	−0.1663[a] (0.0308)	−0.1439[a] (0.0279)	−0.1225[a] (0.0275)
$\ln MANU_t$	−0.0561 (0.0821)	−0.0578 (0.0801)	−0.0011 (0.0763)	0.2746[a] (0.0605)	0.2293[a] (0.0618)	0.2813[a] (0.0596)
R-squared	0.7581	0.7775	0.7929	0.8997	0.8912	0.8988
Hausman Test	180.77[a]	177.88[a]	176.26[a]	201.48[a]	192.65[a]	188.79[a]

Note (1) [a], [b], and [c] indicate significance at the 1%, 5%, and 10% levels, respectively. (2) The analysis includes year dummies, but the results are not included for brevity

from the entire sample, we can see that environmental innovation has a more substantial effect on reducing CO_2 emissions in high-income countries than in the overall sample or middle-income countries.

As columns (1)–(3) show, only high-income countries follow the EKC pattern. This is evident from the significant and positive coefficient on GDP per capita and the significant and negative coefficient on the squared term of GDP per capita. The implication is that as income increases, so do CO_2 emissions; however, as income levels continue to improve, this upward trend eventually weakens, shifting downward after a certain threshold. Therefore, we can attribute the inverse U-shape curve observed in high-income countries to the implementation of pollution reduction measures in response to heightened social pressures and increased environmental awareness (Choi and Han 2018).

Next, we can see that trade increases CO_2 emissions in middle-income countries and decreases CO_2 emissions in high-income countries. The implication is that a high degree of trade openness encourages industrial activities that generate CO_2

emissions in middle-income countries. In other words, we can say that the scale effects of trade occur. Our result is consistent with that in several previous studies (Ike et al. 2020; Wang et al. 2019). We find that trade openness reduces CO_2 emissions in high-income countries. It indicates the technological effects of trade openness, which encourages high-income countries to adopt cleaner technologies and engage in environmentally friendly trade. FDI also increases CO_2 emissions in middle-income countries. Specifically, we find that a 1% increase in FDI increases CO_2 emissions by approximately 0.02%. This is consistent with previous studies that suggest that an increase in FDI inflows stimulates economic activity in middle-income Asian countries, leading to economic growth and environmental degradation from increased CO_2 emissions.

In high-income countries, we find that urbanization increases CO_2 emissions. Namely, for a 1% increase in urbanization, CO_2 emissions in these countries increase by approximately 0.9%. Although urbanization has the potential to foster economic progress, the high energy consumption linked to it ultimately results in increased emissions, posing a threat to the environment (Ghazouani 2022; Lin et al. 2017; Liu and Bae 2018).

However, we find that renewable energy consumption in high-income countries has no impact on CO_2 emissions, although it reduces emissions in middle-income countries. This is because, in high-income countries, the level of renewable energy usage is not yet at a point where it can significantly reduce CO_2 emissions. The lnREC for high-income countries is 0.2095, while it is 2.4039 for middle-income countries, indicating a much higher proportion of renewable energy use. Overall, Asian countries have a much lower proportion of renewable energy use than advanced countries, such as those in Europe. Even among high-income Asian countries, the proportion of renewable energy consumption is significantly lower than the average for all high-income countries. Thus, greater efforts are needed in terms of policy and other activities to increase renewable energy use. We also find that manufacturing activities increase CO_2 emissions in high-income countries. This means that for a 1% increase in manufacturing, CO_2 emissions increase in these countries by approximately 0.4%.

Table 8 presents the results of Asian countries classified by the government effectiveness index, where columns (1)–(3) represent high-effectiveness countries and columns (4)–(6) represent low-effectiveness countries. The classification of countries based on government effectiveness shows slightly different results from those based on the income-based classification, as high- and middle-income countries reflect mixed results in each group.

First, environmental innovation has a positive impact on the environment in high-effectiveness countries. The one- and two-year lagged environmental innovation variables, shown in columns (2) and (3), decrease CO_2 emissions in high-effectiveness countries. However, the coefficient on environmental innovation is negative but not statistically significant for low-effectiveness countries. This implies that the effect of environmental innovation on CO_2 emissions varies depending on the effectiveness of the government. This is reflected in the caliber of a government's policy development and implementation, as well as its credibility and commitment to environmental policies. Further, this could imply that in terms of environmental innovation aimed at environmental protection, low-effectiveness countries may not be implementing such technology; while it is being implemented in high-effectiveness countries. The implication is that countries with governments dedicated to higher quality policies aimed at protecting and conserving the environment are more effective than countries less dedicated to such policymaking. Therefore, to reduce environmental degradation, it is important to concentrate not only on environmental innovation but also on political factors, such as policies that support and reinforce it.

We expected to confirm the EKC hypothesis only in countries with high government effectiveness, similar to the income-based trend. However, we show that the EKC is valid for both high- and low-effectiveness countries. In other words, the GDP per capita coefficient is significant and positive value, while the square term of GDP per capita coefficient is significant and negative. This implies that when income increases, CO_2 emissions also increase; however, after a certain income level, the increase weakens and CO_2 emissions begin to decrease.

Trade openness increases CO_2 emissions only in high-effectiveness countries, whereas FDI decreases CO_2 emissions in high-effectiveness countries but increases these in low-effectiveness countries. This indicates that both low- and high-effectiveness countries have yet to adopt trade-related policies aimed at protecting and conserving the environment. Additionally, in the case of FDI in high-effectiveness countries, environmentally friendly technologies introduced by foreign companies promote more efficient resource use and lower CO_2 emissions, thus having a positive impact on domestic CO_2 emissions. However, in low-effectiveness countries, FDI contributes to environmental degradation by promoting industrial activities. Furthermore, inadequate regulations for environmental protection in low-effectiveness countries compared with those of high-effectiveness countries indicates the potential for FDI inflows to cause environmental degradation.

Urbanization increases CO_2 emissions in high-effectiveness countries, while in low-effectiveness countries, it has negative coefficient but this is not statistically significant. This result reflects the presence of a large urban population in developed countries, especially in high-effectiveness countries. However, urbanization increases CO_2 emissions in the full sample. The proportion of renewable energy use decreases CO_2 emissions per capita in low-effectiveness countries. This result is similar to the full sample findings in Table 6.

5 Conclusion

This study analyzes the effects of environmental innovation, represented by environmental patents, and other variables such as trade openness, urbanization and FDI, etc. on CO_2 emissions in Asian countries. We also divide our sample into 10 high-income countries and 16 middle-income countries in Asia, as well as 10 high-effectiveness and 16 low-effectiveness countries, to investigate the influence of environmental innovation on CO_2 emissions reduction.

Our main results are as follows. First, we find that environmental innovation reduces CO_2 emissions in high-income, middle-income, and high-effectiveness countries, but not in low-effectiveness countries. Environmental innovation has a greater impact on reducing CO_2 emissions in high-income countries than in middle-income countries and in high-effectiveness countries than in low-effectiveness countries. Second, regarding the EKC hypothesis, when grouping by income, the hypothesis is valid only in high-income countries, while grouping by government effectiveness shows the presence of the EKC hypothesis in both groups. Third, in the entire sample, trade openness and FDI do not show significant effects. However, both trade openness and FDI have significant effects in the subsample analyses. Specifically, trade openness decreases carbon emissions in high-income countries and increases CO_2 emissions in middle-income countries. In terms of government effectiveness, trade openness increases CO_2 emissions only in high-effectiveness countries. Additionally, FDI increases CO_2 emissions in middle-income countries, while looking at government effectiveness, it has a negative relationship with CO_2 emissions in high-effectiveness, but increase CO_2 emissions in low-effectiveness countries. Fourth, renewable energy use decreases CO_2 emissions in middle-income and low-effective countries. However, in high-income and high-effectiveness countries, renewable energy use does not reach the levels needed to substantially reduce CO_2 emissions. Finally, urbanization shows positive coefficients on CO_2 emissions in high-income and high-effectiveness countries, whereas manufacturing shows positive coefficients in high-income and low-effectiveness countries.

Obviously, this study confirms that environmental innovation is key to reducing CO_2 emissions. Economic growth and government effectiveness are also vital for environmental protection. In particular, the government's role is important because the government must cooperate to support technology innovation and green growth in order to increase eco-friendly energy. Our findings are significant because they reveal a link between environmental innovation and CO_2 emissions in Asian countries, a topic that has not been previously investigated.

References

Adams, S., and A.O. Acheampong. 2019. "Reducing carbon emissions: The role of renewable energy and democracy." Journal of Cleaner Production 240.

Ahmad, M., M. Shabir, R. Naheed, and K. Shehzad. 2022. "How do environmental innovations and energy productivity affect the environment? Analyzing the role of economic globalization." International Journal of Environmental Science and Technology 19:7527–7538.

Ahmad, M., P. Jiang, A. Majeed, M. Umar, Z. Khan, and S. Muhammad. 2020. "The dynamic impact of natural resources, technological innovations and economic growth on ecological footprint: An advanced panel data estimation." Resources Policy 69.

Al-Mulali, U., H.F. Gholipour, and S.A. Solarin. 2022. "Investigating the environmental Kuznets curve (EKC) hypothesis: Does government effectiveness matter? Evidence from 170 countries." Environment, Development & Sustainability 24:12740–12755.

Atasoy, B.S. 2017. "Testing the environmental Kuznets curve hypothesis across the U.S.: Evidence from panel mean group estimators." Renewable & Sustainable Energy Reviews 77:731–747.

Cheng, C., X. Ren, Z. Wang, and C. Yan. 2019. "Heterogeneous impacts of renewable energy and environmental patents on CO2 emission - Evidence from the BRIICS." Science of the Total Environment 668:1328–1338.

Choi, J.Y., and D.B. Han. 2018. "The links between environmental innovation and environmental performance: Evidence for high- and middle-income countries." Sustainability (Switzerland) 10.

Cramer, W., J. Guiot, M. Fader, J. Garrabou, J.-P. Gattuso, A. Iglesias, M.A. Lange, P. Lionello, M.C. Llasat, S. Paz, J. Peñuelas, M. Snoussi, A. Toreti, M.N. Tsimplis, and E. Xoplaki. 2018. "Climate change and interconnected risks to sustainable development in the Mediterranean." Nature Climate Change 8:972–980.

Danish, and R. Ulucak. 2020. "How do environmental technologies affect green growth? Evidence from BRICS economies." Science of the Total Environment 712.

OECD Data: Air and GHG emissions. https://data.oecd.org/air/air-and-ghg-emissions.htm

Dauda, L., X. Long, C.N. Mensah, and M. Salman. 2019. "The effects of economic growth and innovation on CO2 emissions in different regions." Environmental Science and Pollution Research 26:15028–15038.

Dauda, L., X. Long, C.N. Mensah, M. Salman, K.B. Boamah, S. Ampon-Wireko, and C.S. Kofi Dogbe. 2021. "Innovation, trade openness and CO2 emissions in selected countries in Africa." Journal of Cleaner Production 281.

Du, L., C. Wei, and S. Cai. 2012. "Economic development and carbon dioxide emissions in China: Provincial panel data analysis." China Economic Review 23:371–384.

Du, K., P. Li, and Z. Yan. 2019. "Do green technology innovations contribute to carbon dioxide emission reduction? Empirical evidence from patent data." Technological Forecasting & Social Change 146:297–303.

Fatima, N., Z. Yanting, and N. Guohua. 2023. "Interrelationship among environmental policy stringency, financial globalization in OECD countries, and CO2 emission with the role of technological innovation and financial development." Environmental Science and Pollution Research 30:34085–34100.

Fernández, F.Y., M.A.F. López, and B.O. Blanco. 2018. "Innovation for sustainability: The impact of R&D spending on CO2 emissions." Journal of Cleaner Production 172:3459–3467.

Gani, A., and F. Scrimgeour. 2014. "Modeling governance and water pollution using the institutional ecological economic framework." Economic Modelling 42:363–372.

Ghazouani, T. 2022. "The Effect of FDI Inflows, Urbanization, Industrialization, and Technological Innovation on CO2 Emissions: Evidence from Tunisia." Journal of the Knowledge Economy 13:3265–3295–3295.

Global Carbon Project. https://www.globalcarbonproject.org/

Gormus, S., and M. Aydin. 2020. "Revisiting the environmental Kuznets curve hypothesis using innovation: new evidence from the top 10 innovative economies." Environmental Science and Pollution Research 27:27904–27913.

Handoyo, R.D., Y. Rahmawati, S.F. Ahsani, O.G.R. Altamirano, A.K. Hudang, and T. Haryanto. 2022. "An empirical investigation between FDI, tourism, and trade on CO2 emission in Asia: Testing Environmental Kuznet Curve and Pollution Haven Hypothesis." International Journal of Energy Economics and Policy 12:385–393–393.

Hashmi, R., and K. Alam. 2019. "Dynamic relationship among environmental regulation, innovation, CO2 emissions, population, and economic growth in OECD countries: A panel investigation." Journal of Cleaner Production 231:1100–1109.

Hausman, J.A. 1978. "Specification Tests in Econometrics." Econometrica 46:1251–1271.

IEA. https://www.iea.org/reports/world-energy-outlook-2018

Ike, G.N., O. Usman, and S.A. Sarkodie. 2020. "Testing the role of oil production in the environmental Kuznets curve of oil producing countries: New insights from Method of Moments Quantile Regression." Science of the Total Environment 711.

Khan, M., and A.T. Rana. 2021. "Institutional quality and CO2 emission–output relations: The case of Asian countries." Journal of Environmental Management 279.

Lin, S., S. Wang, D. Marinova, D. Zhao, and J. Hong. 2017. "Impacts of urbanization and real economic development on CO2 emissions in non-high income countries: Empirical research based on the extended STIRPAT model." Journal of Cleaner Production 166:952–966.

Liu, X., and J. Bae. 2018. "Urbanization and industrialization impact of CO2 emissions in China." Journal of Cleaner Production 172:178–186.

Mehmood, U. 2023. "Analyzing the role of political risk, GDP, and eco-innovations towards CO2 emissions in South Asian countries." Journal of the Knowledge Economy:1–15.

Mert, M., and A.E. Caglar. 2020. "Testing pollution haven and pollution halo hypotheses for Turkey: a new perspective." Environmental Science and Pollution Research 27:32933–32943.

Milindi, C.B., and R. Inglesi-Lotz. 2022. "The role of green technology on carbon emissions: does it differ across countries' income levels?" Applied Economics 54:3309–3339–3339.

Mohd Suki, N., N. Mohd Suki, S. Afshan, A. Sharif, M. Ariff Kasim, and S. Rosmaini Mohd Hanafi. 2022. "How does green technology innovation affect green growth in ASEAN-6 countries? Evidence from advance panel estimations." Gondwana Research 111:165-173

Mongo, M., F. Belaïd, and B. Ramdani. 2021. "The effects of environmental innovations on CO2 emissions: Empirical evidence from Europe." Environmental Science and Policy 118:1–9.

Nair, M., M.B. Arvin, R.P. Pradhan, and S. Bahmani. 2021. "Is higher economic growth possible through better institutional quality and a lower carbon footprint? Evidence from developing countries." Renewable Energy 167:132–145.

Nasrullah, N., M.I.u. Husnain, and M.A. Khan. 2023. "The dynamic impact of renewable energy consumption, trade, and financial development on carbon emissions in low-, middle-, and high-income countries." Environmental Science and Pollution Research 30:56759–56773.

Naz, A., and M. Aslam. 2023. "Green innovation, globalization, financial development, and CO2 emissions: the role of governance as a moderator in South Asian countries." Environmental Science and Pollution Research 1–20.

Pata, U.K., M.M. Dam, and F. Kaya. 2023. "How effective are renewable energy, tourism, trade openness, and foreign direct investment on CO 2 emissions? An EKC analysis for ASEAN countries." Environmental science and pollution research international 30:14821–14837.

Saleem, H., M.B. Khan, and S.M. Mahdavian. 2022. "The role of green growth, green financing, and eco-friendly technology in achieving environmental quality: Evidence from selected Asian economies." Environmental Science and Pollution Research 29: 57720–57739.

Sebri, M., and O. Ben-Salha. 2014. "On the causal dynamics between economic growth, renewable energy consumption, CO2 emissions and trade openness: Fresh evidence from BRICS countries." Renewable and Sustainable Energy Reviews 39:14–23.

Sharma, S.S. 2011. "Determinants of carbon dioxide emissions: Empirical evidence from 69 countries." Applied Energy 88:376–382.

Su, H.-N., and I.M. Moaniba. 2017. "Does innovation respond to climate change? Empirical evidence from patents and greenhouse gas emissions." Technological Forecasting & Social Change 122:49–62.
Tan, W., and T. Cao. 2023. "Can green technology reduce carbon dioxide emissions? Evidence from G7 and BRICS countries." Heliyon 9.
Tiba, S., and A. Omri. 2017. "Literature survey on the relationships between energy, environment and economic growth." Renewable & Sustainable Energy Reviews 69:1129–1146.
To, A.H., D.T.T. Ha, H.M. Nguyen, and D.H. Vo. 2019. "The impact of foreign direct investment on environment degradation: Evidence from emerging markets in Asia." International Journal of Environmental Research and Public Health 16.
Töbelmann, D., and T. Wendler. 2020. "The impact of environmental innovation on carbon dioxide emissions." Journal of Cleaner Production 244.
Usman, O., A.A. Alola, and S.A. Sarkodie. 2020. "Assessment of the role of renewable energy consumption and trade policy on environmental degradation using innovation accounting: Evidence from the US." Renewable Energy 150:266–277.
Wang, Y., X. Sun, and X. Guo. 2019. "Environmental regulation and green productivity growth: Empirical evidence on the Porter Hypothesis from OECD industrial sectors." Energy Policy 132:611–619.
Wen, J., W. Ali, J. Hussain, N.A. Khan, H. Hussain, N. Ali, and R. Akhtar. 2022. "Dynamics between green innovation and environmental quality: new insights into South Asian economies." Economia Politica: Journal of Analytical and Institutional Economics 39:543–565.
Wijethilake, C., R. Munir, and R. Appuhami. 2018. "Environmental innovation strategy and organizational performance: enabling and controlling uses of management control systems." Journal of Business Ethics 151:1139–1160.
World Bank. (2021). Government effectiveness, https://datacatlog.worldbank.org/government-effectiveness-estimate
Yıldırım, D.Ç., Ö. Esen, and S. Yıldırım. 2022. "The nonlinear effects of environmental innovation on energy sector-based carbon dioxide emissions in OECD countries." Technological Forecasting & Social Change 182.
Zhang, N., K. Yu, and Z. Chen. 2017. "How does urbanization affect carbon dioxide emissions? A cross-country panel data analysis." Energy Policy 107:678–687.

The Contribution of Migrant Inventors to Environmental Innovation in the Asia-Pacific Region

Ivan Etzo and Sumiko Takaoka

1 Introduction

Over the past decades, countries in the Asia-Pacific region have been achieving economic growth through innovation. Along with economic expansion, human mobility has become a worldwide phenomenon. At the same time, common global problems persist, such as environmental and energy challenges and natural disasters. Moreover, as globalization and regional economic development have advanced, these problems have increased. Against this backdrop, accelerating innovation in environmental technologies can be a promising means of achieving sustainable development. While climate change effects are increasingly challenging the planet, the overall world's creation of new technologies is highly concentrated among the top inventor countries. In fact, between 1990 and 2011, these countries account for approximately 57% of the world's total patent applications in environment-related technologies (Haščič and Migotto 2015). Specifically, the OECD countries account for 88.8% of these applications, the European Union (EU28) 26.8%, and the BRICS 6.9% (see Haščič and Migotto 2015, Table 5, p. 28).

In this context, the current literature points to the role of highly skilled migrants in technology diffusion and innovation. Accordingly, this chapter explores the role of international migrant inventors in environmental technology knowledge diffusion and innovation. Specifically, we focus on the nexus between these inventors and environmental innovation in the Asia-Pacific region. The nexus covers traditional innovative countries, such as the US and Japan, as well as emerging innovative countries, such as China, India, and South Korea. Following the same overall patent pattern, the

I. Etzo (✉)
Department of Economics and Business and CRENoS, University of Cagliari, Cagliari, Italy
e-mail: ietzo@unica.it

S. Takaoka
Faculty of Business Administration, Seikei University, Tokyo, Japan
e-mail: takaoka@bus.seikei.ac.jp

S. Takaoka (ed.), *Environmental Technology Innovation and ESG Investment*,
https://doi.org/10.1007/978-981-99-9768-8_6

creation of new technologies (Keller 2004) and innovation in environment-related technology (ENV-tech) is highly concentrated in a few countries (Haščič and Migotto 2015). This high concentration is a characteristic of current global innovation. As such, there are several interesting and important trends worth noting. First, notwithstanding the overall growth in all innovation activity (the twofold number of patent applications in 2011 compared with 1990), those in environment-related technologies are the fastest-growing (more than a threefold increase between 1990 and 2011). Second, there has been a constant drop in patent activity concentration in this field, with a sharp decline in the shares of the top three inventor countries. To gain a better understanding of what these trends mean, we need to investigate the main drivers of innovation in environment-related technologies.

Research and development (R&D) investment is an important source of innovation (Stephan 2010). However, increasing R&D expenditure on environmental technology may not be sufficient to change the path of technology (e.g., from "dirty" to "clean" innovation). One reason is that technological innovation is a path-dependent process, as its main inputs, research and knowledge production, are also path-dependent (Aghion et al. 2019; Singh and Agrawal 2011). Inventors' knowledge is, to some extent, tacit, making technology only partially codified, and thus not easily transferable (Polanyi 1958). Ultimately, technology diffusion requires that inventors and scientists work together in the same geographic location (Keller 2004; David 1992).[1]

One strand of the literature shows that networks of high-skilled migrants with degrees and occupations in science, technology, engineering, and mathematics (STEM) increase international knowledge diffusion (Miguelez and Noumedem Temgoua 2020; Ganguli 2015; Gaulé and Piacentini 2013; Stephan and Levin 2001), scientific productivity (Gaulé and Piacentini 2013), the stock of human capital, and patenting (Kerr and Lincoln 2010; Hunt and Gauthier-Loiselle 2010; Kerr and Lincoln 2010).[2] Recent studies have focused on migrant inventors, a particular subset of high-skilled migrants, representing a fundamental input for innovation production. Bahar et al. (2020) use the stock of international inventors compiled by Miguelez and Fink (2017) to analyze the impact of migrant inventors on the dynamics of patent applications for a large panel of countries for the years 1990, 2000, and 2010. They find that migrant inventors induce patenting activity (in both sending and receiving countries) in the same technologies that the (sending or receiving) country has a relative advantage in. Ferrucci (2020) finds that Soviet inventors who migrated to Germany following the collapse of the Soviet Union increased German patent

[1] Other important channels of technology diffusion that have been identified in the literature include trade and foreign direct investment (FDI). Keller (2004) notes that imports represent a significant channel of technology diffusion, whereas the evidence for benefits associated with exports is weaker. Bahar et al. (2014) find that the growth rate of exports will increase at 1.5% per annum if the neighboring country has a comparative advantage in existing products. Aitken and Harrison (1999) show the positive correlation between inward FDI and domestic firm productivity.

[2] Park (2004) and Le (2010) empirically show that migrant workers as well as international students serve as channels for R&D spillovers. In terms of openness, the channels of innovation and technology diffusion across countries are discussed both theoretically by Buera and Oberfield (2020) and empirically by Ortega and Peri (2014).

production in technologies that the Soviet Union had previously specialized in. He also finds that collaboration between Soviet- and German-based inventors increased the technology diversion of the latter. Using inventor-level data Moser et al. (2014) find that German Jewish émigrés encouraged chemical innovation in the US in the fields of the émigrés, with patenting by US inventors increasing by 31%. Other studies confirm that the international migration of inventors boosts innovation with immigrant inventors being more productive than native-born inventors (Akcigit et al. 2017; Pellegrino et al. 2023; Franzoni et al. 2014). However, the empirical literature lacks studies analyzing the relationship between migrant inventors and environmental innovation, particularly in the Asia-Pacific region. To fill this gap in the literature, we conduct an empirical analysis of the effects of migrant inventors on the production of new environment-related technologies in the Asia-Pacific region.

To measure innovation performance, we use patent application data in the environment-related technologies as developed by the OECD's Directorate for Science, Technology and Industry. Haščič et al. (2015) thoughtfully point out that patent inventions are particularly suited to study environmental innovation for several reasons. First, by definition, patents are a measure of innovation. Second, they represent innovation output, although an intermediate one. Third, they facilitate the identification of specific environmental aspects. Last, patent data are accessible at the global level, and long time-series are available as well.[3]

Undoubtedly, there is no perfect measure of innovation per se. As pointed out by Haščič et al. (2015), it is important to select an appropriate innovation indicator based on the study objective. Accordingly, we use the patent family size of two or more; that is, patents filed at least at two patent offices among the five largest intellectual property offices in the world (IP5). The five patent offices are: the US Patent and Trademark Office (USPTO), the European Patent Office (EPO), the Japan Patent Office (JPO), the Korean Intellectual Property Office (KIPO), and the National Intellectual Property Administration (CNIPA formerly SIPO) in China.

This indicator is particularly suitable for cross-country analyses in narrow technological fields (for a discussion, see Haščič et al. 2015). Moreover, indicators based on patent family size allow for control over the quality of innovation output. In other words, this measure can be viewed as the quantity of self-selected valuable innovation. The inventor decides to protect intellectual property in more than one jurisdiction only if the patent has potentially high economic value. Thus, claimed priorities can be viewed as representing inventions of higher value because patenting is costly (for a discussion, see Haščič and Migotto 2015).[4]

[3] Other alternative measures are as follows: R&D expenditure and/or employment in R&D (see, e.g., Zacchia 2020; Bottazzi and Peri 2007), although these represent inputs in the innovation production process. Total factor productivity (TFP) growth is used to measure the overall innovation output, but it does not allow to disentangle the different technological aspects of the innovation activity (see, e.g., Peri 2012; Ortega and Peri 2014; Buera and Oberfield 2020).

[4] Possible indicators for the quantity of innovation output include the number of patent applications, granted patents, and bibliometric data (i.e., scientific publications). Those measuring the quality of innovation output include forward citation measures. However, the bibliometric data are intermediate output indicators of innovation and ambiguous indicators of market output.

Increased number of patent applications and the rise in patent shares of the countries in the Asia-Pacific region suggest that more countries are shifting their technological paths toward environmental technology innovation. We investigate the variation in these environmental innovation activities across Asia-Pacific countries looking at changes in inventor migration and other determinants of innovation. Similar to Bahar et al. (2020), we assume that innovation is favored by immigrant (emigrant) inventors originating from (residing in) countries specialized in environmental technology. As a measure of technology specialization, we use the revealed technological advantage (RTA) based on Soete (1987) and Bahar et al. (2020).

The international mobility of inventors is not measured directly by publicly available statistics. However, proper indicators can be constructed by leveraging patent data (see Miguelez and Fink 2017, for a discussion). We use the disambiguated inventor database constructed by Pellegrino et al. (2023) to create the migrant inventor variables. Pellegrino et al. (2023) use machine learning techniques to identify inventors across patents uniquely and ultimately track the migration patterns of nearly one million individual inventors across countries.[5] The main advantage of using this novel inventor database is that it avoids the double counting problem and reduces measurement errors. In other words, foreign inventors in the same country could be counted multiple times. Both issues are highlighted by Bahar et al. (2020), who use the stock of migrant inventors compiled by Miguelez and Fink (2017).

Results of our ordinary least squares (OLS) analysis suggest that innovation in environment-related technologies increases with the stock of immigrant inventors. The point estimates indicate that a 10% increase in immigrant inventors raises the environmental patent applications of the host country by 1.7–2.8% (depending on model specification). The estimates of the dynamic model confirm the main results and are consistent with the path-dependent characteristic of innovation.

To address the endogeneity concerns regarding the causal impact of migrant inventors on environment technology innovation, we conduct two tests. First, we employ the instrumental variable (IV) estimation technique to address endogeneity concerns arising from possible measurement errors and reverse causality. Indeed, countries that increase innovation activity also become more attractive to foreign inventors. We construct our instrument by applying the approach used by Bahar et al. (2020) for a similar analysis. Our main results show that a 10% increase in immigrant inventors raises the host country's environmental patent applications by 2.7–4.1% (depending on model specification). Immigrant inventors still have a positive, economically meaningful, and statistically significant impact on environmental technology innovation. Second, we conduct a falsification test to confirm that innovation is indeed triggered by inventors from countries specializing in environment-related innovation. Robustness analysis confirms the main outcomes.

The results for the controls are also noteworthy. First, we find robust evidence that innovation in environment-related technologies increases with the number of natural disasters in each country. Second, environmental innovation also increases with the CO_2 emissions per capita.

[5] Detailed data can be found in Pellegrino et al. (2023).

Our study contributes to the literature in three ways. First, we extend the recent literature on migrant inventors and innovation by showing that inventor mobility is also an important factor in shaping paths toward environmental technology innovation. Second, we add to the vast literature on international migration and innovation diffusion by showing that the migration of inventors from countries specializing in environment-related technology is important for increasing environmental innovation activity in destination countries. Finally, our analysis contributes to the literature on the main drivers of environmental innovation for sustainable development in the Asia-Pacific region. Namely, we show that, besides migrant inventors, environmental technology innovation increases with CO_2 emissions and the number of natural disasters.

The remainder of this chapter is organized as follows. Section 2 describes trends in environmental patents, inventors, and their distribution across Asia-Pacific countries. Section 3 explains our empirical strategy for identifying the relationship between migrant inventors and environmental technology innovation. Section 4 describes the data in our empirical analysis. Section 5 presents the empirical results. The final section concludes.

2 Patterns and Trends of Environmental Innovation and Migrant Inventors in the Asia-Pacific Region

In this section, we describe the patterns and trends of environmental innovation, representing relatively new technology, and those of migrant inventors in the Asia-Pacific region.

2.1 Environmental Technology Production in the Asia-Pacific Region

In our study, we use patent data to measure innovation output because patent data are widely applied to represent technology categories and quantity of innovation output. Moreover, they have two important advantages over other commonly used indicators, such as R&D expenditure and the number of scientific personnel in industries. The first is that patents measure the intermediate outputs of the inventive process, whereas R&D and scientific personnel measure the inputs of innovation. Another advantage is that patent data are widely available, and can be disaggregated into specific technological fields (Haščič et al. 2015; Breschi et al. 2014). However, patents also present some challenges: not all innovations are patentable (e.g., organizational, managerial, and nontechnological innovations); patents are not the only way to protect innovation; thus, not all patentable inventions are patented. In addition, patented inventions vary in terms of quality. Thus, a mere count of patents ignores innovation quality. In this

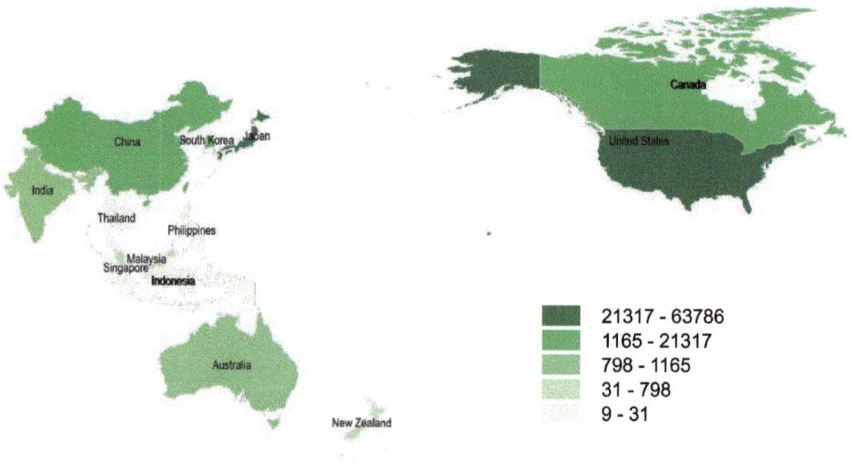

Fig. 1 Environment patent applications (year: 2012) *Notes* The darker the green shading, the larger the number of environmental patent applications as of 2012 by countries in the Asia-Pacific region

regard, a way to control the quality of patents is to consider only patent applications claimed as "priority" in more than one jurisdiction. Patent applications, granting, and renewal imply high costs for applicants; thus, potential low-value inventions usually seek protection solely at a single patent office (Haščič and Migotto 2015; Guellec and van Pottelsberghe 2000). We implicitly assume that applicants distinguish the value of their innovations and apply for only valuable innovations in more than one patent office. Therefore, as stated above, we count only the number of patents filed in at least two patent offices among the five largest intellectual property offices in the world (IP5).

Figure 1 shows the inventor countries for environmental patent creation in the Asia-Pacific region. The US and Japan have traditionally been innovative countries ranked as the top two inventor countries in the world over in the past. While these two countries remain highly innovative in the world, Table 1 in Chap. 1 shows that China, South Korea, and Singapore rapidly increased their number of environmental patent applications. A notable feature of Asia-Pacific countries is that they include both traditional and emerging inventor countries. This implies that environmental technology creation is geographically dispersed, with an increasing global share of environmental technology patent applications within the Asia-Pacific region. More importantly, the Asia-Pacific region represents a core group of innovative countries that are contributing to sustainable development worldwide.

Figure 2 shows the share of environmental technology patent applications in applicant countries. New Zealand and Australia are the top two countries enthusiastic about creating environmental technology. Traditional inventor countries, such as the US and Japan, are also creating a relatively high share of environmental technologies.

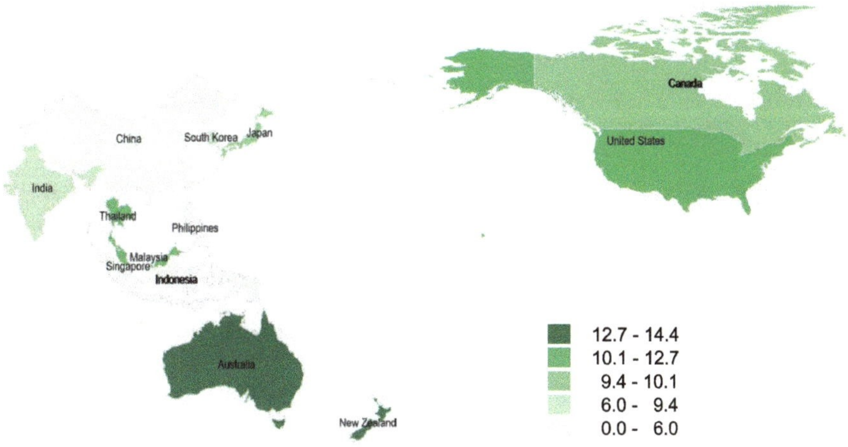

Fig. 2 Environment patent applications shares (year: 2012) *Notes* This figure shows the share of environment patent application to total patent applications in the countries in the Asia-Pacific region. The darker the green shading, the higher the share of environmental patent applications within a country as of 2012 in the Asia-Pacific region

As environmental technology is a comparatively new technology category, Fig. 3 shows an upward trend in the environment patent growth rate since the mid-2000s across applicant countries—most notably the growth rate in India. In addition to India, traditional inventor countries, such as the US and Japan, have maintained steady growth. Emerging innovative countries, such as China, India, Singapore, and South Korea, have shown a high growth rate in environmental technology creation since the reference year 1990. This implies that the Asia-Pacific region represents a core of environmental technology creation globally.

Looking at the environmental patent applications by category for each country, Fig. 4 presents the environmental technology categories for a patent application: capture, storage, sequestration, or disposal of greenhouse gases; climate-change mitigation technologies in the production or processing of goods; climate-change mitigation technologies related to buildings; climate-change mitigation technologies related to energy generation, transmission, or distribution; climate-change mitigation technologies related to transportation; climate-change mitigation technologies related to wastewater treatment or waste management; environmental management; and water-related adaptation technologies. Note that, according to the OECD, the count of "selected environment-related technologies" is less or equal to the sum of its sub-components (environmental management, climate-change mitigation). This is because patents are commonly classified into multiple technology classes. Therefore, each patented invention is counted only once when aggregated across technological domains. Thus, the sum of category shares exceeds 100% for most countries in Fig. 4.

The composition of technology categories is distinct among countries; for example, traditional inventor countries, such as the US and Japan, cover all categories in

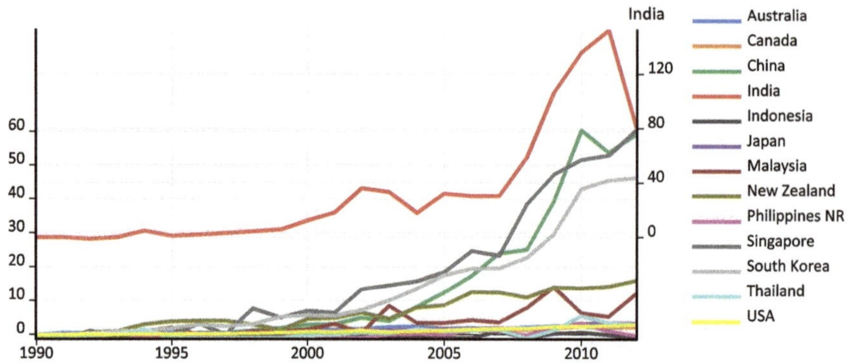

Fig. 3 Environment patents trends (base year: 1990) *Notes* This figure plots the time-series growth rate of the environmental patent applications (base year = 1990). The right axis indicates the rate of environmental patent growth for India, whereas the left axis indicates the rate for the rest of the countries in the Asia-Pacific region

the patent applications. In contrast, some countries, such as Indonesia, cover specific technology categories. The US and Canada show relatively similar patterns of technology composition in patent applications. Australia and New Zealand are both green innovative countries in their overall patent applications, but their environmental technology categories do not show the same pattern. Technology categories common to the countries in Fig. 4 are "Climate-change mitigation technologies related to energy generation, transmission or distribution" and "Environmental management."

In sum, countries in the Asia-Pacific region have been fostering environmental technology innovation worldwide; in particular, emerging inventor countries have been accelerating innovation in environmental technologies. Thus, this region is playing a key role in achieving sustainable growth worldwide and will continue to do so in the near future.

2.2 *Migrant Inventors in the Asia-Pacific Region*

Migrant inventors have attracted attention in the recent literature because they are a subset of high-skilled migrants who contribute to innovation in destination countries. Furthermore, spillover effects through the network of migrant inventors are expected to affect innovation activities in the home countries.

Our study uses data on international migrant inventors created by Pellegrino et al. (2023). Figure 5 shows the trend of destination countries for migrant inventors in the Asia-Pacific region; that is, the number of immigrant inventors engaged in technology creation in this region. Note that data on migrant inventors created by Pellegrino et al. (2023) are from patent application data. Hence, international migrant inventors who never applied for patents are not counted as migrant inventors in our study.

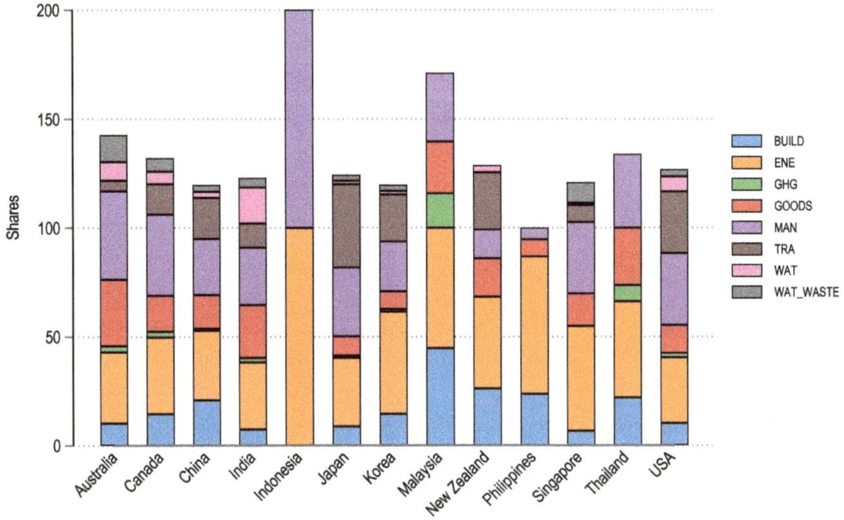

Fig. 4 Share of environmental patent applications by category (year: 2012) *Notes* To illustrate the composition of the technology category, this figure shows the share of patent applications in the environmental technology category: Capture, storage, sequestration or disposal of greenhouse gases; climate change mitigation technologies in the production or processing of goods; climate change mitigation technologies related to buildings; climate change mitigation technologies related to energy generation, transmission or distribution; climate change mitigation technologies related to transportation; climate change mitigation technologies related to wastewater treatment or waste management; environmental management; and water-related adaptation technologies. Note that, according to OECD, the count of "selected environment-related technologies" is less or equal to the sum of its sub-components (environmental management, climate change mitigation). This is because patents are commonly classified in more than one technology class. Therefore, each patented invention is counted only once when aggregating across technological domains. For this reason, the sum of the category shares exceeds 100% for most of the countries in Fig. 4

The largest host country for international migrant inventors is the US, with a huge gap between it and the second-largest host country. To some degree, we see an upward trend in immigrant inventors across countries, suggesting that skilled migrants, particularly migrant inventors, are more mobile and dispersed geographically, at least in the Asia-Pacific region.

Figure 6 shows that China is the largest sending country of emigrant inventors; with a big gap between it and India, the second-largest sending country. Both China and India are emerging as innovative countries in terms of number of patent applications. The implication is that human capital for innovation is actively moving within Asia-Pacific countries, and that such migrant inventors are contributing to innovation in destination countries.

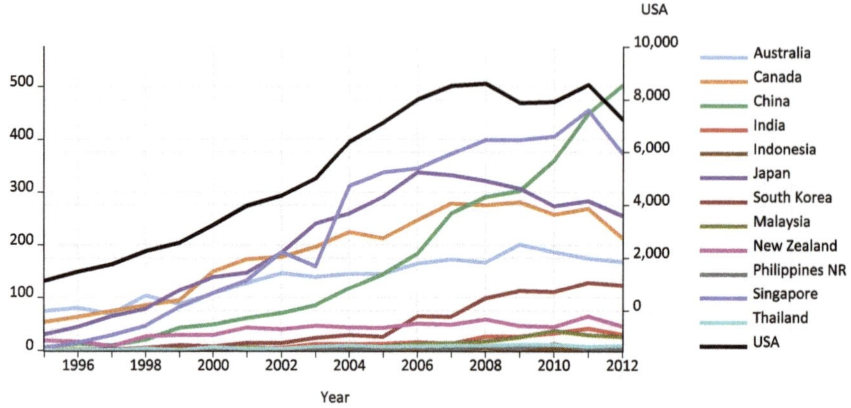

Fig. 5 Trend of immigrant inventors *Notes* This figure plots the time-series data of immigrant inventors in the destination country from 1995 through 2012. The right axis indicates the number of immigrant inventors in the US, whereas the left axis indicates that for the rest of the countries in the Asia-Pacific region. *Source* Data created by Pellegrino et al. (2023)

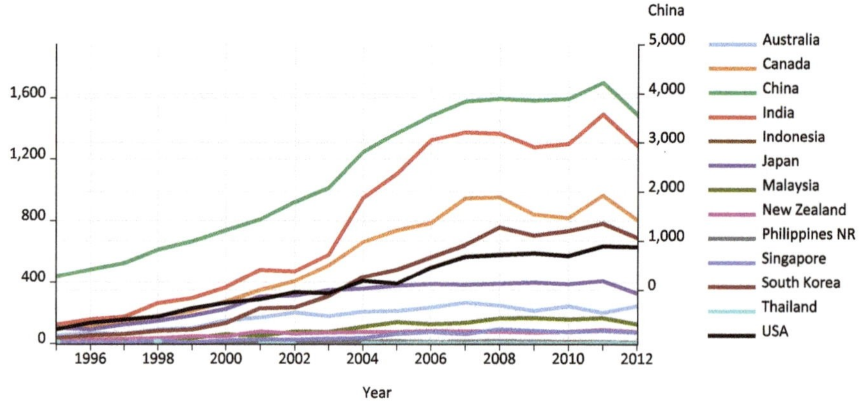

Fig. 6 Trend of emigrant inventors *Notes* This figure plots the time-series data of emigrant inventors who are originally from a country in the Asia-Pacific region from 1995 through 2012. The right axis indicates the number of emigrant inventors from China, whereas the left axis indicates that for the rest of the countries in the Asia-Pacific region. *Source* Data created by Pellegrino et al. (2023)

2.3 *The Relationship Between Environmental Patents and Migrant Inventors*

This subsection illustrates the relationship between environmental patents and migrant inventors in the Asia-Pacific region. Figure 7 plots the growth of environmental patent applications and immigrant inventors. The green circle in the figure indicates the total number of patents based on yearly average growth rates for 1990–

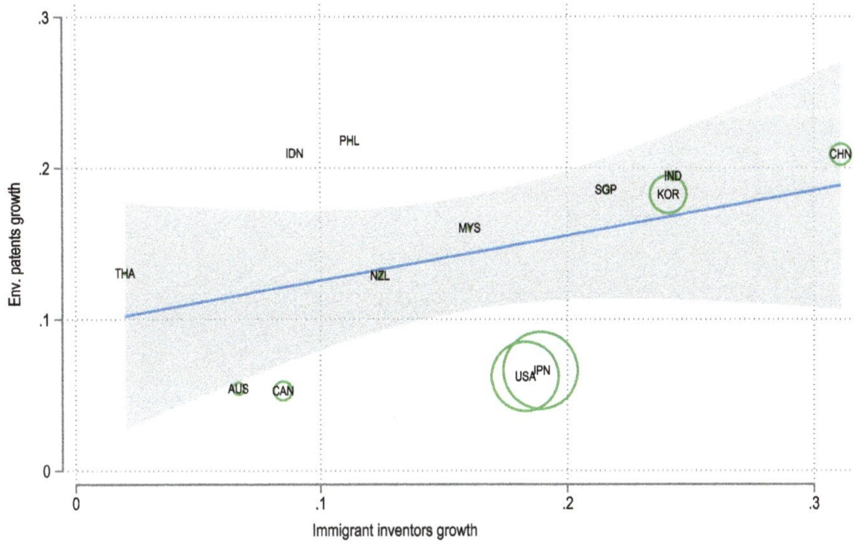

Fig. 7 Immigrant inventor and environmental patents *Notes* The figure plots the growth of environment patent applications along with the growth of immigrant inventors. The size of the green circle indicates the number of total patents. Yearly average growth rates are for the period 1990–2012. The blue line represents the simple regression line with the 95% confidence interval in gray

2012. The simple regression line suggests a positive relationship between the increase in immigrant inventors and the growth of environmental patents.

When we look at the total number of immigrant inventors, the US is the largest receiving country. However, when consider the growth of immigrant inventors over time, China, India, and South Korea, which are emerging inventive countries, show a higher growth rate of immigrant inventors. This indicates that they are not only sending countries of migrant inventors but also receiving countries in recent years.

Figure 8 plots the growth in environmental patent applications along with that of emigrant inventors, where the green circle indicates the total number of patents. These are based on the annual average growth rates for 1990–2012. In contrast to Fig. 7, the simple regression line in Fig. 8 is almost horizontal, suggesting no sign of a relationship. If we focus on countries with a large number of patent applications, such as the US, Japan, South Korea, and China, at the same time, they represent high emigrant inventor growth within the Asia-Pacific region. There appears to be a positive relationship between emigrant inventors and environmental patent growth in these countries.

This section illustrates what the stylized facts tell us about trends in environmental innovation and migrant inventors in the Asia-Pacific region. The next section carefully and empirically examines this relationship using the RTA index in environment-related technology.

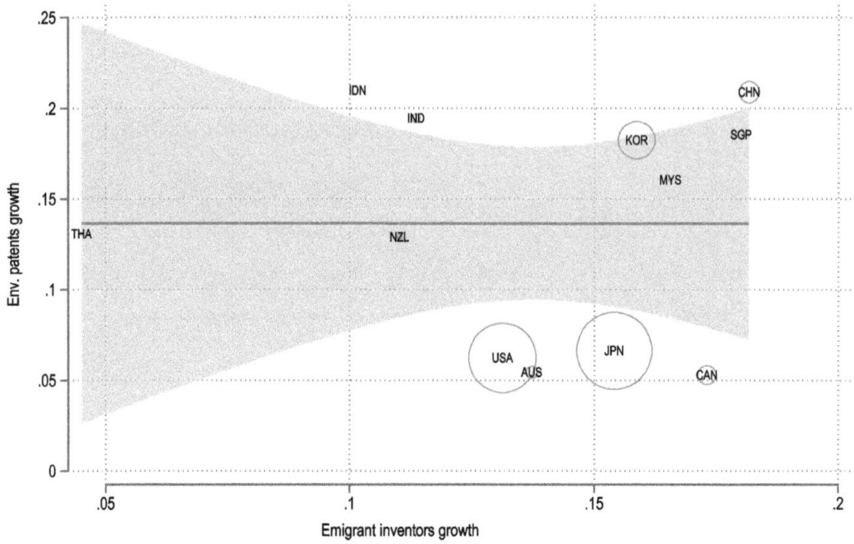

Fig. 8 Emigrant inventor and environmental patents *Notes* The figure plots the growth of environment patent applications along with the growth of emigrant inventors. The size of the green circle indicates the number of total patents. Yearly average growth rates are for the period 1990–2012. The blue line represents the simple regression line with the 95% confidence interval in gray

3 Empirical Strategy

3.1 Empirical Specification

We adopt an innovation production framework, drawing on several studies in the literature (Mairesse and Mohnen 2002; Furman et al. 2002; Buesa et al. 2010; Ponds et al. 2009). This approach assumes that a country's innovation performance arises from a generalized production function, expressed as follows:

$$y_{it} = f(x_{it}, u_{it}) \tag{1}$$

In this equation, y_{it} represents the innovation output of country i in year t and x_{it} is a vector of inputs expected to contribute to innovation. The term u_{it} can be viewed as the unexplained ability to innovate Mairesse and Mohnen (2002). Notably, Mairesse and Mohnen (2002) apply an accounting framework to compare innovation performance across seven European countries and refer to the residual term of the innovation function as "innovativeness."

As our analysis aims to investigate the influence of migrant inventors on environmental innovation in the Asia-Pacific region, we need to specify appropriate measures for the relevant variables. Accordingly, we measure innovation output y_{it} by examining the number of patent applications from country i in year t. Specifically, we focus on patent applications in environment-related technology categories ($j = 1, 2, .., 8$), as categorized by OECD Search Strategies for the Identification of Selected Environment-Related Technologies (Haščič and Migotto 2015).[6]

For our primary explanatory variables, we concentrate on migrant inventors originating from countries in the Asia-Pacific region that specialize in specific environment-related technologies (j). Immigrant inventors from such specialized countries are expected to have valuable tacit knowledge, potentially enhancing the innovation performance of the destination country in the same environment-related technology (j). Similarly, sending countries may benefit from valuable knowledge spillover, because emigrant inventors reside in countries specialized in environment-related technology (j).

To identify countries specializing in environment-related technology (j), we use the RTA index introduced by (Bahar and Rapoport 2018; Bahar et al. 2020). The environmental technology patenting RTA index for country i for environment-related technology j and year t ($RTA^{envtech}_{i,j,t}$) is computed using the following formula:

$$RTA^{envtech}_{i,j,t} = \frac{envpat_{i,j,t} \Big/ y_{i,t}}{\sum_i envpat_{i,j,t} \Big/ \sum_i y_{i,t}} \tag{2}$$

Here, $envpat_{i,j,t}$ represents the number of patent applications in the environment-related technology category j for country i in year t.

To construct the annual stock of immigrant inventors originating from countries in the Asia-Pacific region who specialize in environment-related technology j for each country i, we use the following formula:

$$imminv_{i,j,t} = \sum_s inventors^{im}_{i,s,t} \times ES_{s,j,t}, \tag{3}$$

where $s \neq i$ denotes the origin country of the immigrants, i is the destination country, and $ES_{s,j,t}$ is a dummy variable taking the value 1 if $RTA^{envtech}_{s,j,t} \geqq 1$, and 0 otherwise.

Similarly, to compute the stock of emigrant inventors originating from country i and residing in countries specialized in environment-related technology j, we use the following formula:

$$eminv_{i,j,t} = \sum_s inventors^{em}_{i,s,t} \times ES_{s,j,t}, \tag{4}$$

where $i \neq s$ and $ES_{s,j,t} = 1$ if $RTA^{envtech}_{s,j,t} \geqq 1$, and 0 otherwise.

Having outlined our main empirical strategy and defined the outcome and response variables, we now specify a complete econometric model. Our primary specification

---

[6] The OECD search strategy covers approximately 80 technological fields, and the eight environmental categories encompass various areas, such as greenhouse gas capture, climate-change mitigation technologies, and environmental management.

for studying the effects of migrant inventors on patent applications for environment-related technologies is given by the following equation:

$$envpat_{ijt} = \beta_0 + \beta_{im} imminv_{i,j,t-3} + \beta_{em} eminv_{i,j,t-3} + \gamma x_{i,t-3} + \lambda trade_{i,j,t-3} + \alpha_{ij} + \phi_t + \varepsilon_{ijt} \quad (5)$$

Here, $x_{i,t-3}$ represents a vector of country-level control variables, including R&D expenditure, CO_2 emissions, and the number of natural disasters. We expect innovation output to increase with R&D expenditure, measured as overall public and private R&D expenditure as a percentage of GDP. As concerns about air pollution, which are closely linked to the earth's climate and ecosystems globally, are relevant, we include CO_2 emissions per capita among the control variables. Additionally, we control for historical natural disasters because extreme events can hasten the urgency of environmental technology innovation activity. Furthermore, we explore the impact of international trade as a channel for technology diffusion by constructing the variable $trade_{i,j,t-3}$ using the similar weighting scheme applied to the migration variables.

Finally, to account for country- and time-specific effects, we include technology-by-country fixed effects (α_{ij}) and year fixed effects (ϕ_t).

In the analysis, all variables, except "the number of disasters," undergo a linear monotonic transformation using the inverse hyperbolic sine (Burbidge et al. 1988). This allows the estimated coefficients for the transformed regressors to be interpreted as elasticities.

3.2 Instrumental Variables

Our primary variables of interest are not fully exogenous as there may be unobservable time-varying country-technology characteristics that influence both inventor migration destination choices and the dynamics of environmental patents. To address potential endogeneity issues, we use the two-stage least squares (2SLS) method to estimate the econometric model in Equation (5). Following Bahar et al. (2020), we construct instruments for the number of immigrant and emigrant inventors.

Specifically, we use inventor data to compute the push and pull factors for each pair of countries, i (receiving country) and s (sending country).[7] The push factor for country s is defined as the share of emigrant inventors from country s to all destination countries d (excluding country i):

$$PUSH_{s,t}^{-i} = \frac{\sum_d inv_{s,d,t}}{\sum_d \sum_s inv_{s,d,t}}, \quad \text{where} \quad d \neq i \quad (6)$$

[7] A similar approach has been used by Burchardi et al. (2018) in their study of migration's effect on FDI.

Similarly, the pull factor for country i is the share of total immigrant inventors in country i from all other countries of origin o (excluding country s).

$$PULL_{i,t}^{-s} = \frac{\sum_o inv_{i,o,t}}{\sum_o \sum_i inv_{i,o,t}}, \quad \text{where} \quad o \neq s \tag{7}$$

Using push and pull factors, we predict the bilateral stock of inventor migrants between countries i and s as follows:

$$IVinv_{i,s,t} = PUSH_{s,t}^{-i} \times PULL_{i,t}^{-s} \times \sum_i \sum_s inv_{i,s,t} \tag{8}$$

Finally, we construct instruments using the same weighting scheme applied to compute the migrant inventor variables. Hence, the instruments for immigrant and emigrant inventors specialized in environment-related technology j are computed as:

$$ETInvIV_{i,j,t}^{m} = \sum_s IVinv_{i,s,t} \times ES_{s,j,t} \tag{9}$$

where m represents either immigrants or emigrants depending on whether the instrument is computed for immigrant or emigrant inventors from country i specialized in environment-related technology j.

In sum, by excluding countries s and i from the construction of the push and pull factor variables, respectively, we ensure that our instruments are exogenous to the production of environmental technology patents. The first-stage results in Sect. 5.2 demonstrate that our instruments are good predictors of the migrant inventor variables.

4 Data

Environmental innovation activity is measured by the number of patent applications filed by country i for environment-related technology j during 1990-2011. As discussed, we consider patent family size as the measure of patent quality and focus on inventions with a family size of two or greater (higher-value patents seeking protection in at least two jurisdictions). The analysis covers eight categories of environment-related technologies shown in Fig. 4.

Data on international migrant inventors come from Pellegrino et al. (2023). Their dataset provides information on inventors listed in patent applications filed under the PCT administered by the WIPO, spanning 1978 to 2012. A notable advantage of this database is the unique identifiers for disambiguated inventors. Key variables, such as nationality (citizenship) and residence, enable the identification of migrant inventors.

It is important to note that the identification of migrant inventors relies solely on distinguishing between the country of residence and citizenship (data on country of birth are unavailable). Consequently, our sample of migrant inventors includes inventors with dual nationality and non-movers, as information on the year of migration is not accessible. Nevertheless, both types of (long-term) migrant inventors are significant for our empirical investigation, as they are likely to maintain connections with both their country of origin and destination (e.g., through collaborative work and social networks), facilitating the transfer of innovation knowledge between these nations.

The control variables in our regression model include gross domestic expenditure on R&D (as a % of GDP), CO_2 emissions per capita, the number of natural disasters, and international trade. Data on R&D expenditures (as a % of GDP) come from the UNESCO database. CO_2 emission data (metric tons per capita) come from the World Bank data bank. The number of natural disasters per country comes from the Emergency Events Database (EM-DAT) provided by the Centre for Research on the Epidemiology of Disasters (CRED) at the Catholic University of Louvain.[8] Countries more susceptible to natural disasters are expected to prioritize safety measures, including safety management, preparation, and prevention, which can spur innovation in environment-related technologies aimed at natural disaster prevention and mitigation. Finally, data for the international trade variable come from the Atlas of Economic Complexity Dataverse the Harvard Dataverse Repository.

Descriptive statistics are presented in Table 1. As mentioned, both the cross-country and within-country standard deviations of patent applications are substantial. The same applies to the two variables representing the stock of migrant inventors, which are the primary regressors of interest. Notably, we see considerable variation in the stock of international trade and number of natural disasters. The latter statistics are unsurprising, given that certain countries are frequently affected by natural disasters, whereas others experience such events less frequently.

5 Empirical Results

In this section, we first assume that all regressors are exogenous. The results of the OLS estimates are presented in Table 2. In the first specification, we assume that the production of environment-related technologies is determined by R&D expenditure, CO_2 emissions, and the number of natural disasters. In addition to these regressors, we control for unobserved country-specific, environment-related technology fixed effects, and year-specific effects (column (1)). All the estimated coefficients are statistically significant, although the point estimates for R&D expenditure and

[8] The EM-DAT is a global database on natural and technological disasters, encompassing data from 1900 to the present. Recorded disasters in EM-DAT meet at least one of the following criteria: 10 or more people dead, 100 or more people affected, the declaration of a state of emergency, or a call for international assistance.

Table 1 Descriptive statistics

		Mean	Std. dev.	Min	Max	N/n/$\bar{T}$
Number of environmental patents	Overall	91.11	280.54	0.00	2653.62	2271.00
	Between	–	240.06	0.00	1533.79	104.00
	Within	–	137.69	−652.18	1693.43	21.84
Emigrant inventors	Overall	271.02	698.09	0.00	5115.00	2129.00
	Between	–	496.84	0.00	2341.91	103.00
	Within	–	471.22	−2054.89	3044.11	20.67
Immigrant inventors	Overall	231.48	790.72	0.00	6991.00	2044.00
	Between	–	598.49	0.00	3408.57	104.00
	Within	–	465.74	−3109.09	3813.91	19.65
GERD as a % of GDP	Overall	1.91	0.79	0.56	3.85	1367.00
	Between	–	0.71	0.76	2.95	72.00
	Within	–	0.32	1.08	3.28	18.99
CO_2 emission per capita	Overall	8.13	6.13	0.64	20.47	2271.00
	Between	–	6.04	0.85	19.00	104.00
	Within	–	0.98	4.60	11.47	21.84
Number of natural disasters	Overall	15.35	18.58	0.00	101.00	2271.00
	Between	–	16.89	0.09	65.06	104.00
	Within	–	7.83	−21.72	58.69	21.84
Trade (Billion US$)	Overall	157.00	222.37	1.79	1455.80	2271.00
	Between	–	185.24	5.60	913.63	104.00
	Within	–	120.53	−319.60	990.39	21.84

the number of natural disasters are not very precise. In column (2), we add our variables of interest, namely, the stock of immigrant and emigrant inventors. Both variables positively impact the number of patent applications in environment-related technologies. The results do not change substantially when we control for the effect of international trade in column (3), although the estimated coefficient for the latter is not statistically significant. In the last column of Table 2 we add a lagged dependent variable. The estimated coefficient is positive and statistically significant, indicating the presence of path dependence in environmental technology innovation. The esti-

Table 2 OLS results

	OLS—environmental patents			
	(1)	(2)	(3)	(4)
R&D exp.	0.731[c]	0.027	0.038	−0.042
	(0.432)	(0.374)	(0.374)	(0.222)
CO_2 emissions	1.837[a]	1.564[a]	1.367[a]	0.620[a]
	(0.349)	(0.305)	(0.375)	(0.233)
Disasters	0.006[c]	0.004	0.003	0.004[c]
	(0.003)	(0.003)	(0.003)	(0.002)
Emig. inventors		0.197[b]	0.187[b]	0.093[c]
		(0.083)	(0.083)	(0.048)
Immig. inventors		0.280[a]	0.271[a]	0.166[a]
		(0.059)	(0.062)	(0.041)
Trade			0.163	0.123
			(0.234)	(0.143)
Patents (lagged)				0.457[a]
				(0.047)
Observations	1172	1157	1157	1152
R^2	0.67	0.69	0.69	0.76

Notes Robust standard errors clustered by country and patents' sub-category in parentheses. All regressors are lagged by three years. Country by patents' sub-category fixed effects, and year dummies are included. [a] significant at 1%, [b] significant at 5%, [c] significant at 10%

mated (positive) effect of immigrant inventors remains highly statistically significant throughout the specifications. A 10% increase in the number of immigrant inventors increases applications for patents in environment-related technologies by approximately 17% (column (4)). By contrast, the estimated impact of emigrant inventors in their country of origin is smaller, and the point estimates are less precise when the lagged dependent variable is included.

As for the other determinants, the OLS results are as follows. Increased CO_2 emissions are likely to stimulate the development of clean technologies. The results remain robust across all specifications, suggesting that a 1% increase in CO_2 emissions per capita leads to a 1.4% increase in green patent applications (full model in column (3)). The impact of the number of natural disasters is positive and statistically significant only in the first and final models. The estimated coefficient of the trade variable exhibits the expected positive sign but is not statistically significant.

In sum, the OLS estimates suggest that migrant inventors promote environmental innovation, although the estimated impact is greater and statistically more robust for immigrant inventors than for emigrant inventors. However, because we acknowledge potential endogeneity concerns, we apply the IV estimation technique in the subsequent section to obtain consistent coefficients for our main variables of interest.

Table 3 IV first-stage results

	The dep. var. is immig. inv. for models 1-3-5-7 and emig. inv. for models 2-4-6-8							
	(1)	(2)	(3)	(4)	(5)	(6)	(7)	(8)
Immig. inventors (instr.)	0.312[a] (0.023)	0.039[b] (0.019)	0.806[a] (0.025)	0.261[a] (0.027)	0.793[a] (0.025)	0.254[a] (0.028)	0.759[a] (0.026)	0.233[a] (0.029)
Emig. inventors (instr.)	0.055[b] (0.025)	0.262[a] (0.018)	0.141[a] (0.025)	0.266[a] (0.027)	0.126[a] (0.024)	0.258[a] (0.028)	0.121[a] (0.024)	0.253[a] (0.028)
R&D exp.			1.976[a] (0.171)	0.143 (0.116)	1.969[a] (0.165)	0.140 (0.117)	1.892[a] (0.165)	0.100 (0.118)
CO_2 emissions			−0.929[a] (0.108)	0.258[a] (0.082)	−1.323[a] (0.147)	0.055 (0.107)	−1.418[a] (0.149)	−0.016 (0.108)
Disasters			−0.013[a] (0.001)	0.002[b] (0.001)	−0.014[a] (0.001)	0.001 (0.001)	−0.013[a] (0.001)	0.002[c] (0.001)
Trade					0.321[a] (0.087)	0.165[a] (0.058)	0.290[a] (0.088)	0.152[a] (0.058)
Patents(lagged)							0.042[c] (0.024)	0.035[c] (0.019)
Observations	1787	1787	1157	1157	1157	1157	1152	1152

Notes Robust standard errors clustered by country and patents' sub-category in parentheses. All regressors are lagged by three years. Country by patents' sub-category fixed effects, and year dummies are included. [a] significant at 1%, [b] significant at 5%, [c] significant at 10%

5.1 IV Results

We begin the discussion of the 2SLS estimation by presenting the outcomes of the first stage in Table 3. The instruments we use as instrumental variables are described in Sect. 3.2. Columns (1), (3), (5), and (7) show the first-stage outcomes when the dependent variable is the number of immigrant inventors. Similarly, in columns (2), (4), (6), and (8), the dependent variable is the number of emigrant inventors. Columns (5) and (6) present the first-stage results corresponding to the model specifications in column (3) of Table 2. The last two columns report the dynamic specification results (column (4) of Table 2). The F-test rejects the null hypothesis of weak instrumental variables at the 1% level across all specifications for both the immigrant and emigrant variables.

Besides the instruments, the findings suggest substantial correlations between some regressors and the variables measuring migrant inventors. As expected, countries that increase their R&D expenditure attract more immigrant inventors. An increase in CO_2 emissions makes the country less attractive for immigrant inventors and increases the outflow. Similar results emerge for the number of natural disasters. Natural disasters act as push factors for domestic inventors and discourage others from moving in. International trade is positively associated with immigration and emigrant inventors. The results are robust to the inclusion of lagged dependent variables.

Table 4 IV results

	IV—environmental patents			
	(1)	(2)	(3)	(4)
Immig. inventors	0.335[a]	0.405[a]	0.407[a]	0.272[a]
	(0.073)	(0.070)	(0.070)	(0.059)
Emig. inventors	−0.004	0.026	−0.002	−0.065
	(0.093)	(0.130)	(0.130)	(0.112)
R&D exp.		−0.162	−0.164	−0.189
		(0.266)	(0.267)	(0.234)
CO_2 emissions		1.605[a]	1.427[a]	0.676[a]
		(0.172)	(0.211)	(0.196)
Disasters		0.005[b]	0.004[c]	0.005[b]
		(0.002)	(0.002)	(0.002)
Trade			0.151	0.119
			(0.117)	(0.095)
Patents(lagged)				0.450[a]
				(0.036)
Observations	1787	1157	1157	1152
R^2	0.52	0.66	0.66	0.73
Kleibergen-Paap underid.	123.40	32.17	30.24	29.74
p-val	0.00	0.00	0.00	0.00
Kleibergen-Paap weak id.	118.77	24.27	23.50	23.04

Notes Robust standard errors clustered by country and patents' sub-category in parentheses. All regressors are lagged by three years. Country by patents' sub-category fixed effects, and year dummies are included. [a] significant at 1%, [b] significant at 5%, [c] significant at 10%

Table 4. The effect of immigrant inventors is positive and statistically significant across different model specifications. A 10% increase in immigrant inventors increases the number of patent applications for environment-related technologies by approximately 4% (3% after controlling for the path-dependence effect). The impact of emigrant inventors appears with a negative sign in three out of the four estimates, but is not statistically significant. It is likely that these positive effects do not counterbalance the loss of inventors who are extremely important; especially in developing countries in the Asia-Pacific region. R&D expenditure is not statistically significant and appears to be negative. One possible explanation is that firms find investing in "green" technologies riskier or more difficult than investing in "dirty" technologies. As a result, innovation in "dirty" technologies absorbs most of the R&D expenditure. Two environmental variables, namely, CO_2 emissions and the number of natural disasters, positively influence the production of environmental technology innovation. Bilateral international trade with countries specialized in producing environment-related technologies has a positive sign, but is not statistically significant. All the results are robust to the inclusion of a lagged dependent variable (column (6)).

5.2 Robustness

In this subsection, we use the baseline model specification in Eq. (5) to conduct a falsification experiment on the weighting scheme implemented to construct our principal regressors and the international trade variable.

The objective of the falsification test is to validate the independence of our findings from pre-existing trends in migrant inventors or unaccounted for variables. We adjust the weighting scheme so that the construction of the migrant inventor variables includes only individuals from countries that lack specialization in environment-related technologies. Mathematically, we modify the indicator variable $ES_{s,j,t}$ in Eqs. (3) and (4) so that it assumes a value of one when $RTA^{envtech}_{s,j,t} < 1$ and zero otherwise.

The outcomes reported in Table 5 demonstrate that the impact on environmental technology patent applications is not statistically significant when considering immigrant inventors originating from countries without specialization in environment-

Table 5 Falsification test

	IV—environmental patents			
	(1)	(2)	(3)	(4)
Immig. inventors	−0.036 (0.065)	−0.099 (0.074)	−0.076 (0.076)	−0.020 (0.041)
Emig. inventors	0.028 (0.082)	0.037 (0.090)	0.038 (0.086)	−0.068 (0.073)
R&D exp.		0.590[b] (0.267)	0.577[b] (0.265)	0.227 (0.231)
CO_2 emissions		1.768[a] (0.176)	1.385[a] (0.225)	0.541[a] (0.202)
Disasters		0.007[a] (0.002)	0.006[b] (0.002)	0.005[b] (0.002)
Trade			0.302[a] (0.111)	0.179[b] (0.091)
Patents(lagged)				0.519[a] (0.037)
Observations	1273	1061	1061	1057
R^2	0.57	0.66	0.66	0.75
Kleibergen-Paap underid.	10.83	10.68	10.78	10.81
p-val	0.00	0.00	0.00	0.00
Kleibergen-Paap weak id.	56.07	64.89	64.32	64.97

Notes Robust standard errors clustered by country and patents' sub-category in parentheses. All regressors are lagged by three years. Country by patents' sub-category fixed effects, and year dummies are included. *** significant at 1%, ** significant at 5%, * significant at 10%

related technology innovation j. The findings for the remaining regressors closely resemble those observed in Table 2, except for international trade, which is now statistically significant.

6 Conclusions

Using environmental technology patent data and migrant inventor data created by Pellegrino et al. (2023), this chapter provides evidence of a positive and significant relationship between immigrant inventors and environmental technology innovation in the Asia-Pacific region. Immigrant inventors are helping countries achieve sustainable development by increasing innovation in environmental technology. This result holds when other patent-application production factors are controlled. To address potential endogeneity concerns, we use an instrumental variable approach. The statistical significance of the relationship between immigrant inventors and environmental technology innovation is robust to the use of instrumental variables.

The main results indicate that a 10% increase in immigrant inventors increases the host country's environmental technology patent applications by 2.7% (the preferred model specification). The other determinants are that environmental technology innovation increases with air pollution (i.e., CO_2 emissions) and the number of natural disasters. The estimates of the dynamic model confirm that our results are consistent with the path-dependence characteristic of innovation in the literature.

We also conduct the falsification test to confirm that innovation is indeed triggered by immigrant inventors from countries specialized in environment-related innovation. Consistent with the results obtained through the OLS and the instrumental variable methods, the falsification test shows that immigrant inventors from countries that do not specialize in environment-related innovation do not affect the environmental patent applications of the destination country. In conclusion, our results are robust to the potential endogeneity of the main regressors, different model specifications, and the falsification test on the weighting scheme used to consider only the migration of inventors from countries specialized in environmental technology innovation.

Our results provide important findings with many implications for academic research and policymaking in relatively new environmental technology. For example, we broadly agree that climate change, particularly global warming, is an emergent and global problem; however, we need to accelerate environmental technology innovation activities, given the time lags of innovation input on output. For example, to foster environmental technology innovation, a special visa policy for environmental technology scientists or inventors could facilitate inventor mobility across countries and global technology transmission for sustainable development. Other measures to boost innovation activities using international inventor network could also help disseminate technology to mitigate climate change and achieve sustainable development.

References

Aghion, P., H. Cameron, A. Teytelboym, and D. Zenghelis (2019). Path dependence, innovation and the economics of climate change. In R. Fouquet (Ed.), *Handbook on Green Growth*, Chapter 4, pp. 67–83. Edward Elgar Publishing.

Aitken, B. J. and A. E. Harrison (1999). Do domestic firms benefit from direct foreign investment? Evidence from Venezuela. *The American Economic Review 89*(3), 605–618.

Akcigit, U., J. Grigsby, and T. Nicholas (2017). Immigration and the rise of American ingenuity. *American Economic Review 107*(5), 327–331.

Bahar, D., P. Choudhury, and H. Rapoport (2020). Migrant inventors and the technological advantage of nations. *Research Policy 49*(9), 103947.

Bahar, D., R. Hausmann, and C. A. Hidalgo (2014). Neighbors and the evolution of the comparative advantage of nations: Evidence of international knowledge diffusion? *Journal of International Economics 92*(1), 111–123.

Bahar, D. and H. Rapoport (2018). Migration, knowledge diffusion and the comparative advantage of nations. *The Economic Journal 128*(612), F273–F305.

Bottazzi, L. and G. Peri (2007). The international dynamics of R&D and innovation in the long run and in the short run. *The Economic Journal 117*(518), 486–511.

Breschi, S., F. Lissoni, and G. Tarasconi (2014). Inventor data for research on migration and innovation: A survey and a pilot. WIPO Economics & Statistics Series, Economic Research Working Paper No. 17.

Buera, F. J. and E. Oberfield (2020). The global diffusion of ideas. *Econometrica 88*(1), 83–114.

Buesa, M., J. Heijs, and T. Baumert (2010). The determinants of regional innovation in Europe: A combined factorial and regression knowledge production function approach. *Research Policy 39*(6), 722–735.

Burbidge, J. B., L. Magee, and A. L. Robb (1988). Alternative transformations to handle extreme values of the dependent variable. *Journal of the American Statistical Association 83*(401), 123–127.

Burchardi, K. B., T. Chaney, and T. A. Hassan (2018). Migrants, ancestors, and foreign investments. *The Review of Economic Studies 86*(4), 1448–1486.

David, P. A. (1992). Knowledge, property, and the system dynamics of technological change. *The World Bank Economic Review 6*(suppl_1), 215-248.

Ferrucci, E. (2020). Migration, innovation and technological diversion: German patenting after the collapse of the Soviet Union. *Research Policy 49*(9), 104057.

Franzoni, C., G. Scellato, and P. Stephan (2014). The mover's advantage: The superior performance of migrant scientists. *Economics Letters 122*(1), 89–93.

Furman, J. L., M. E. Porter, and S. Stern (2002). The determinants of national innovative capacity. *Research Policy 31*(6), 899–933.

Ganguli, I. (2015). Immigration and ideas: What did Russian scientists "bring" to the United States? *Journal of Labor Economics 41*(2), 450–474.

Gaulé, P. and M. Piacentini (2013). Chinese graduate students and U.S. scientific productivity. *Review of Economics and Statistics 95*(2), 698-701.

Guellec, D. and B. van Pottelsberghe (2000). Applications, grants and the value of patent. *Economics Letters 69*(1), 109–114.

Haščič, I. and M. Migotto (2015). Measuring environmental innovation using patent data. OECD Environment Working Papers No. 89.

Haščič, I., J. Silva, and N. Johnstone (2015). The use of patent statistics for international comparisons and analysis of narrow technological fields. OECD Science, Technology and Industry Working Papers 2015/05.

Hunt, J. and M. Gauthier-Loiselle (2010). How much does immigration boost innovation? *American Economic Journal: Macroeconomics 2*(2), 31–56.

Keller, W. (2004). International technology diffusion. *Journal of Economic Literature 42*(3), 752–782.

Kerr, W. R. and W. F. Lincoln (2010). The supply side of innovation: H-1B visa reforms and U.S. ethnic invention. *Journal of Labor Economics 28*(3), 473-508.

Le, T. (2010). Are student flows a significant channel of R&D spillovers from the north to the south? *Economics Letters 107*(3), 315–317.

Mairesse, J. and P. Mohnen (2002). Accounting for Innovation and Measuring Innovativeness: An Illustrative Framework and an Application. *American Economic Review 92*(2), 226–230.

Miguelez, E. and C. Fink (2017). *Measuring the International Mobility of Inventors: A New Database*, pp. 114-161. Intellectual Property, Innovation and Economic Development. Cambridge University Press.

Miguelez, E. and C. Noumedem Temgoua (2020). Inventor migration and knowledge flows: A two-way communication channel? *Research Policy 49*(9), 103914. STEM migration, research, and innovation.

Moser, P., A. Voena, and F. Waldinger (2014). German Jewish Émigrés and US invention. *American Economic Review, 104*(10), 3222–3255.

Ortega, F. and G. Peri (2014). Openness and income: The roles of trade and migration. *Journal of International Economics 92*(2), 231–251.

Park, J. (2004). International student flows and R&D spillovers. *Economics Letters 82*(3), 315–320.

Pellegrino, G., O. Penner, E. Piguet, and G. de Rassenfosse (2023). Productivity gains from migration: Evidence from inventors. *Research Policy 52*(1), 104631.

Peri, G. (2012). The effect of immigration on productivity: Evidence from U.S. states. *Review of Economics and Statistics 94*(1), 348-358.

Polanyi, M. (1958). *Personal Knowledge: Towards a Post-Critical Philosophy*. Chicago: University of Chicago Press.

Ponds, R., F. v. Oort, and K. Frenken (2009). Innovation, spillovers and university-industry collaboration: an extended knowledge production function approach. *Journal of Economic Geography 10*(2), 231–255.

Singh, J. and A. Agrawal (2011). Recruiting for ideas: How firms exploit the prior inventions of new hires. *Management Science 57*(1), 129-150.

Soete, L. (1987). The impact of technological innovation on international trade patterns: The evidence reconsidered. *Research Policy 16*(2-4), 101–130.

Stephan, P. E. (2010). The economics of science. In B. H. Hall and N. Rosenberg (Eds.), *Handbook of the Economics of Innovation*, Volume 1, Chapter 5, pp. 217–273. North-Holland.

Stephan, P. E. and S. G. Levin (2001). Exceptional contributions to US science by the foreign-born and foreign-educated. *Population Research and Policy Review 20*(1/2), 59–79.

Zacchia, P. (2020). Knowledge spillovers through networks of scientists. *Review of Economic Studies 87*(4), 1989–2018.

GPSR Compliance
The European Union's (EU) General Product Safety Regulation (GPSR) is a set of rules that requires consumer products to be safe and our obligations to ensure this.

If you have any concerns about our products, you can contact us on

ProductSafety@springernature.com

In case Publisher is established outside the EU, the EU authorized representative is:

Springer Nature Customer Service Center GmbH
Europaplatz 3
69115 Heidelberg, Germany

www.ingramcontent.com/pod-product-compliance
Ingram Content Group UK Ltd.
Pitfield, Milton Keynes, MK11 3LW, UK
UKHW022209051026
15624UKWH00001B/83
* 9 7 8 9 8 1 9 9 9 7 6 7 1 *